COUNTERTERRORISM IN WEST AFRICA

The Most Dangerous SAS Assault

WILL FOWLER

ROSEN PUBLISHING

This edition published in 2011 by:

The Rosen Publishing Group, Inc.
29 East 21st Street
New York, NY 10010

Library of Congress Cataloging-in-Publication Data

Fowler, Will, 1947–

Counterterrorism in West Africa: the most dangerous SAS assault/Will Fowler.

   p. cm. — (The most daring raids in history)

Includes bibliographical references and index.

ISBN 978-1-4488-1871-6 (library binding)

1. Sierra Leone—History—Civil War, 1991–2002—Juvenile literature. 2. Operation Barras, 2000—Juvenile literature. 3. Search and rescue operations—
Sierra Leone—Juvenile literature. 4. Great Britain. Army. Special Air Service—Juvenile literature. I. Title.

DT516.826.F678 2011

966.404—dc22

2010029621

Manufactured in the United States of America

CPSIA Compliance Information: Batch #W11YA: For further information, contact Rosen Publishing, New York, New York, at 1-800-237-9932.

Copyright © 2010 Osprey Publishing Limited. First published in paperback by Osprey Publishing Limited.

CONTENTS

INTRODUCTION

Dawn on September 10, 2000, in the West African state and former British colony of Sierra Leone, was the setting for a high-risk hostage rescue operation by men of D Squadron, 22 Special Air Service Regiment (22 SAS) and A Company (A Coy) 1st Battalion The Parachute Regiment (1 Para). The code name for the mission was Operation *Barras*.

The conditions leading up to Operation *Barras* had begun nearly 550 years earlier when the Portuguese maritime explorer Pedro da Cintra, sailing close to Africa's west coast, spotted a serrated jungle-covered mountainous peninsula that loomed out of the surrounding low-lying coastline. It is said that to his crew the feature resembled a crouching lion and so by this association it became *Serra Lyoa* and later *Sierra Leone* – Lion Mountain. The coastline was developed by European slaveowners in the 15th and 16th centuries and for a time the little country was a significant port of exit for slaves destined for the plantations of North America.

The lion-shaped peninsula sheltered an excellent natural harbor which made Sierra Leone an obvious point to break the long seaborne journeys to India and the East before the construction of the Suez Canal, and so the country flourished. In 1787 following the abolition of slavery by the British it was set up as a haven for freed slaves and the name "Freetown" was given to the port at the foot of the mountain. During World War II it was the assembly point for Allied convoys making the hazardous journey through the North Atlantic to the UK.

Sierra Leone has a total land area of 27,698 square miles (71,740 square kilometers), about the size of Scotland or South Carolina. It shares a 90-mile (306 km) land border with Liberia in the east and south-east and a 405-mile (652 km) border with Guinea to the north and north-east. It has a 250-mile (402 km) Atlantic Ocean coastline stretching from the Guinean border in the north-west to the mouth of the Mano River and the Liberian border in the east.

The Freetown Peninsula, the site of the original settlement, is approximately 25 miles (40 km) long and 10 miles (16 km) wide and rises to 328 feet (100 meters) above sea level. At the western end of the peninsula Aberdeen Creek divides the northern Aberdeen Peninsula from greater Freetown. While there were excellent anchorages there was no flat ground to build an airfield so this was constructed at the village of Lungi on the peninsula separated from Freetown by the mouth of the Sierra Leone River. Access to the airfield was by ferry from Freetown to the village of Tangrin and thence by road, or later directly by helicopter. The airport would play a significant part in the evacuation of civilians from Sierra Leone and the rapid movement of troops into the country during operations *Palliser* and *Barras*.

Freetown, the capital and main political and commercial center of Sierra Leone, has the highest population density. Following independence and the outbreak of civil war the population grew as internal refugees flooded in from the surrounding countryside.

At the time the country ceased to be a colony and became independent on April 27, 1961, however, all seemed very promising. Sierra Leone was described as "the Atlantic Switzerland." For a time democracy and the rule of law flourished since the indigenous middle class had enjoyed excellent education both in country, with one school earning the nickname of the Eton of Africa, and at British colleges and universities.

Conflict Diamonds

Sierra Leone is the source of considerable mineral wealth including gem- and industrial-quality diamonds, bauxite (aluminium ore), and

rutile (titanium ore). At the beginning of the 21st century some 450,000 carats of gem-quality and 150,000 carats of industrial-quality diamonds had been produced and gold was also exported in small quantities. This wealth was to be the cause of many of the country's troubles as nepotism and corruption, the latter fuelled by the easy access to diamonds—gems that would eventually be known as "Conflict Diamonds" or "Blood Diamonds"—would drag the country through inflation down to civil war.

A military coup overthrew the civilian government in 1967, and the military were in turn replaced by civilian rule a year later. The country declared itself a republic on April 19, 1971. A coup attempt early in 1971 led to the then prime minister, Siaka Stevens, calling in troops from neighboring Guinea's army, who remained for two years. Stevens turned the government into a one-party state under the aegis of the All People's Congress Party in April 1978. In 1992 rebel soldiers overthrew Stevens' successor, Joseph Momoh, calling for a return to a multiparty system.

In 1991, in the Kailahun District in the Eastern Province, the notoriously brutal Revolutionary United Front (RUF) began an armed campaign against the corrupt government and the military regimes that followed. The RUF had been established in Liberia in the late 1980s by Foday Sankoh, a disaffected army corporal. During 1994, the RUF escalated the guerrilla war and in 1995, when it captured an economically vital rutile mine, the guerrillas controlled most of the countryside.

In 1996, another military coup ousted the country's military leader and president. Nevertheless, a multiparty presidential election proceeded in 1996, and People's Party candidate Ahmad Tejan Kabbah won with 59.4 percent of the vote. The British government signed an agreement with Sierra Leone to train two battalions of the Sierra Leone Army (SLA). This was the basis for the British Army Short Term Training Team (STTT).

A violent military coup ousted Kabbah's government in May 1997. The leader of the coup, Lt. Col. Johnny Paul Koroma, assumed the title Head of the Armed Forces

Freetown, Sierra Leone, at the turn of the 20th century. The view looking north along George Street shows St. George's Cathedral and, beyond it, a British warship at anchor. Freetown would be an important strategic base during both World Wars. (Author's collection)

APRIL 27, 1961

Sierra Leone gains independence.

5

Map of Sierra Leone and neighboring countries.

Revolutionary Council (AFRC). Koroma began a reign of terror, destroying the economy and murdering enemies. The Commonwealth of Nations demanded the reinstatement of Kabbah, and the Economic Community of West African States Monitoring Group (ECOMOG), the Nigerian-led peacekeeping force, intervened in February 1998. In many ways ECOMOG compounded the problems of Sierra Leone with its own corruption, being active in (and later found guilty of) diamond smuggling, theft and extortion.

Opposing Kabbah's forces, members of the ousted military junta known as SOBELs—Soldier Rebels—and the RUF continued to launch attacks accompanied by the terrorising of thousands of civilians including countless children using torture, rape, and brutal amputation by machete. A ghastly humor characterized these amputations—a hand being lopped off was described as a "long sleeve" whereas if the arm were severed at the elbow it was a "short sleeve." The rebels were supported by Liberia's president Charles Taylor who planned to control Sierra Leone's rich diamond fields. On March 10, 1998, after ten months in exile, Kabbah was returned to power following pressure from the international community, notably the United States of America.

In January 1999, when a force composed of the RUF and AFRC with Liberian mercenaries stormed the capital, demanding the release of Sankoh, who had been arrested, it was the beginning of a viciously brutal campaign of terror by the RUF named Operation *No Living Thing*. ECOMOG finally regained control of Freetown, but President Kabbah later released Sankoh so he could participate in peace negotiations. Pressured by Nigeria and the United States of America, among other countries, Kabbah agreed to an untenable power-sharing agreement in July 1999, which made Sankoh vice president of the country—and in charge of the diamond mines. As one observer commented, this appointment was like putting the fox in charge of the hen house.

In October 1999 the UN Security Council passed Resolution 1270 mandating a force of 6,000 peacekeeping troops commanded by Indian general Vijay Kumar Jetley. In many cases Nigerian ECOMOG forces exchanged berets for the blue UN headgear. Other UN troops would come from India and Jordan. In February 2000 the United

Nations Mission in Sierra Leone (UNAMSIL) increased to 11,000 troops and two months later deployed to the 12 districts that made up Sierra Leone.

Despite these large numbers of troops in country the RUF still held the initiative, taking hostages, besieging UN bases and shooting down a UN helicopter. Sankoh, who was now living in Freetown, became the focus of a 30,000-strong mass demonstration by the population against the RUF. His guards opened fire and he made a brief escape before being captured and arrested. Meanwhile, the RUF, a potent and dangerous force in the country, continued attacking and undermining the operations of UNAMSIL.

It was during this fighting that reports circulated of British Special Forces directing the operations of an anti-RUF and, therefore, loosely pro-government group that included former SLA soldiers, in a crucial action at Rogberi Junction, a busy town that had grown up around a former railway junction north of Rokel Creek. The group that styled itself the West Side Boys was "paid" with ammunition, food and medicine. However, the relationship was short-lived because the West Side Boys were reluctant to accept integration into the new SLA that was being formed. Instead, they became what was known euphemistically in Freetown as a group that was "self-provisioning"; in other words, they had become bandits.

Mobilization

In May 2000 the course of events in Sierra Leone would change dramatically as the situation deteriorated. A Zambian battalion, part of UNAMSIL, was reported to have surrendered to the increasingly aggressive and confident RUF. There were fears of a general collapse of UNAMSIL, the capture of Freetown by the RUF and a threat to the safety of the 1,300 Entitled Persons who included UK citizens working in the city. It looked as if it was shaping up to be a repeat of Operation *No Living Thing*. The British Cabinet had met the previous day but at that moment did not wish to take unilateral action fearing that it might precipitate the collapse of UNAMSIL.

On Friday May 5, 1st Battalion The Parachute Regiment (1 Para) was alerted for a possible Non-combatant Evacuation Operation in Sierra Leone. Within the battalion, A Coy was absent in Jamaica on Exercise *Red Stripe*, named after the popular and potent local beer. Their numbers were made up from D Company 2nd Battalion The Parachute Regiment (D Coy) under Maj. Andy Charlton, bringing it up to strength as a Battle Group (BG). The men of A Coy who were disappointed to have missed this operational deployment could not have known that they would play a considerably more significant part in military operations in Sierra Leone later that year.

Once flown out to Sierra Leone the tasks for 1 Para BG, in an operation code-named *Palliser*, were to:

- Establish a HQ at Lungi airfield;
- Secure Lungi and Aberdeen Peninsulas;
- When ordered, secure the British High Commissioner's Residence and compound;
- Establish an Evacuee Assembly Area (EAA) at the UN HQ, Mammy Yoko Hotel and an alternative EAA at Lungi.

Announcements on the BBC World Service and warnings spread via the warden system run by the British High Commission advised the estimated 500 British citizens in and around Freetown to assemble at collection points throughout the city. Most of the evacuees were hoping to cross to the relative safety of Lungi International

1991
RUF begin attacks.

MAY 2000
Operation *Palliser* evacuates threatened civilians.

Soldiers from 1 Para check equipment in front of a Land Rover at Lungi Airport, Freetown, during Operation *Palliser*. C Company Group of 1 Para Battle Group was inserted by air on May 7, 2000, to secure the airport as a forward operating base. (IWM UKLC-2000-049-002-004)

Airport, protected by the 1 Para BG. They were shuttled across by helicopter and while some returned to the UK others waited out the crisis.

The 1 Para BG operations were settling into a steady state by the close of Friday May 12, a week after receiving the first call. The BG was deployed as two groups, the majority around Lungi Airport while D Coy held Aberdeen Peninsula.

The Paras were replaced by a slower-moving but more powerful force, the Amphibious Ready Group (ARG) based around 42 Commando, Royal Marine (42 Cdo) and commanded by Lt. Col. Andy Salmon, which included the Logistic Task Group with their vehicles and communications equipment.

HMS *Ocean*

When the crisis had begun the ARG had been on Exercise *Ambrose Hill* in southern France. At 0200hrs on May 5, it was warned off for possible operations in Sierra Leone. A hastily convened O Group cut short the training and by 0530hrs on May 7 the force was re-embarked and on its way to Gibraltar. Here the Marines fired on the ranges and zeroed their weapons and stores were loaded, and by May 14 HMS *Ocean* (L 12), the ARG flagship, was in position off Sierra Leone.

Besides 42 Cdo, HMS *Ocean* had an Air Group consisting of four Commando Sea Kings Mk 4, two Royal Marine (RM) Air Sqn Lynx Mk 7, two RM Air Sqn Gazelles and two RAF CH47 Chinooks. *Ocean* was a new ship that had entered service in 1999 with a complement of 285 with a further 180 Fleet Air Arm personnel when aircraft were embarked. She could carry up to 800 Royal Marines.

Operation *Palliser* had been a demonstration of the speedy and effective use of military power untrammelled by the UN's Rules of Engagement and complex and inflexible chain of command. It was, therefore, little wonder that the RUF and other militias realized that the forces in Sierra Leone were not to be provoked or humiliated. In the days before the ARG withdrew it was reported that 300 RUF fighters had gathered to surrender but were beyond the 42 Cdo Tactical Area of Operational Responsibility.

JULY 22, 2000

Royal Irish deploy to Sierra Leone as training team.

With the situation secured the Royal Marines withdrew and the STTT got to work at the Benguema Training Centre (BTC) at Waterloo, a village with an airstrip at the southern end of the Freetown Peninsula. Here they would take about 1,000 Sierra Leonean troops through basic training and infantry skills. These men would then form the new SLA 4th Brigade.

In addition to the bases ashore at Freetown harbor, "Percy," the invaluable Royal Fleet Auxiliary (RFA) *Sir Percivale*,[1] was a secure environment in which stores could be kept dry. Detachments were rotated through the RFA and the Quartermaster's working party protected the ship where the soldiers could enjoy respite from the heat and humidity as well as good food. On "Percy" the soldiers from the STTT had a chance to shower, get their kit laundered and sleep in cabins.

The training program began in June with a team from the 2nd Battalion The Royal Anglian Regiment—"The Poachers." They were replaced on July 22 by the 1st Battalion The Royal Irish Regiment (1 RIR). In the months that followed, Sierra Leone attracted a number of high-profile British political visitors keen to be part of a military success story. The success in Africa would shape the British Government's approach to military intervention and eventually lead to Operations *Herrick* and *Tellic*—the invasions of Afghanistan and Iraq.

For the men of 1 RIR—"The Royal Irish"—the tour in Sierra Leone looked as if it would replicate that of the Poachers. Recruits would be interviewed and then medical checks and simple strength and aptitude tests would eliminate some. The process would then begin of taking young men and women and turning them into trained soldiers. Like the Poachers the Royal Irish would also mount vehicle and foot patrols to liaise with UNAMSIL forces and give reassurance to the civilian population.

Men of 1 Para at Lungi airport, Freetown, during Operation *Palliser*. In the background are the four Royal Air Force HC2 Chinook helicopters of No 7 Squadron RAF which played a crucial role in the operation. The Chinooks deployed to Sierra Leone from their base at RAF Odiham with just six hours notice. The flight was the longest in the history of the Chinook, involving a 3,000-mile (4,830 km) flight over three days. (IWM UKLC-2000-049-002-001)

---

1 The Royal Fleet Auxiliary

The primary role of the RFA is to supply the Royal Navy (RN) at sea with the food, fuel, ammunition and spares that it requires in order to maintain operations away from its home ports. In addition, the RFA provides the RN with seaborne aviation training facilities as well as secure logistical support and amphibious operations capability for the Royal Marines and the British Army. In Sierra Leone RFA *Sir Percivale*, which was over 30 years old and a veteran of the Falklands War, could accommodate 340 troops and was fitted with platforms to operate a range of helicopters including Lynx and Chinook.

ORIGINS

In the humid tropical afternoon sunshine of August 25, 2000, in the interior of Sierra Leone a Royal Irish patrol of three Land Rovers, including a Weapons Mount Installation Kit (WMIK, commonly known as a Wimik) fitted with a Browning .50 inch (12.7 mm) heavy machine gun (HMG) and one with a radio, had driven down the dusty red laterite track into the village of Magbeni close to the muddy waters of Rokel Creek in the Occra Hills.

The soldiers in the vehicles from C Company 1 RIR were commanded by Maj. Alan Marshall. The group included the Regimental Signals Officer (RSO) Capt. Flaherty, Company Sergeant Major (CSM) Head, Sgt. Smith, Cpl. Musa Bangura of the SLA, Corporals Sampson, Ryan and Mackenzie and Rangers (Privates) Guant, McVeigh and Rowell.

The patrol had turned off the main road down a long mud track where the oil palms from an abandoned plantation grew close to the verges. They then emerged into open ground, which sloped down to a ferry point across the 900-foot-wide (275m-wide) Rokel Creek with the ruined village of Magbeni stretching for about 656 feet (200 m) down the track in front of them. It was from the village that the crowd of armed West Side Boys unexpectedly appeared.

Among the West Side Boys 22-year-old Ibrahim Koroma recalled the first moments of the encounter with the patrol: "They got down from their vehicles and talked with the boys. We didn't know they were coming, but everything seemed calm."

Preparations for a vehicle patrol using WMIKs—armed Land Rovers—during Operation *Palliser*. Soldiers of 1 Para study a map outside the base of D Company Group in the Aberdeen Peninsula. (IWM UKLC-2000-049-001-033)

The West Side Boys asked Marshall to wait for the return of their leader, the 24-year-old self-styled "Brigadier" Foday Kallay, a former sergeant in the SLA.

At 33 Marshall was one of the youngest majors in the British Army and marked out for a fast track promotion. Under his command the patrol had driven out from their base at Benguema on a liaison visit to Col. Jehad al-Widyan, commanding JordBat 2, the 2nd Jordanian Battalion UNAMSIL at Masiaka. The visit, it would later emerge, had been approved by the Commander British Forces in Sierra Leone and was part of routine liaison with adjacent friendly units to get increased warning of any attack or threat.

Over lunch, Marshall and the other officers had learned from the Jordanians that the West Side Boys were beginning to surrender to the United Nations as part of the disarmament program that had embraced the RUF and other militias. Marshall had diverted his patrol to check this out and to help build up the wider intelligence picture.

Significantly, his was not the first British patrol to visit the area. In the past, the British forces had enjoyed a reasonable working relationship with the loosely structured group. However, when Kallay arrived that afternoon by motorized canoe from his hut in the village of Gberi Bana across the Rokel, the atmosphere changed. He was belligerent and suspicious.

He regarded the area as his territory and was angered because there had been no request for clearance to visit Magbeni. He was probably also feeling aggrieved that his group was beginning to disintegrate with men slipping away to the UN Disarmament Demobilisation and Reintegration (DDR) centers.

AUGUST 25, 2000

West Side Boys ambush and capture RIR patrol.

A paratrooper of 1 Para guards the base of D Company Group and the battle group's headquarters in the Aberdeen Peninsula during Operation *Palliser*. (IWM UKLC-2000-049-001-027)

The group picked up the mood of the youthful, slightly built leader and suddenly became agitated and aggressive. A captured SLA Bedford MK 4.48-ton (4-tonne) truck mounting a twin ZPU-2 14.5mm HMG swung out from behind the huts and blocked the exit south out of the village.[2]

Hostile and armed

The British patrol was now surrounded by a hostile and armed crowd. The Ranger manning the Browning HMG up in the WMIK knew that he could not open fire without killing or wounding his comrades and almost certainly triggering a massacre. However, the radio operator was able to report to the HQ at BTC that they had been surrounded and held against their will.

When Marshall attempted to defuse the tension and then resisted the attempts by West Side Boys to grab his rifle, fists and rifle butts thumped into him and he was badly beaten. This attack on Marshall was a piece of brutal psychology as it sent the message to the rest of the patrol that the West Side Boys did not respect rank and if the commanding officer (CO) could be brutally assaulted—so could they.

Koroma witnessed the brief struggle. "They had no chance to resist," he said. In five minutes the British soldiers were overwhelmed and disarmed. They were stripped down to their olive green T-shirts and underwear; wedding rings and watches were removed and, it was later reported, collected by Kallay. In the first of many increasingly brutal humiliations he put the rings on his fingers and, turning his hands, admired the glitter of the gold in the afternoon sunshine.

The men were forced down to the walled ferry point, bundled into two motorized canoes and taken north upstream across Rokel Creek to Gberi Bana, Kallay's headquarters and the militia's base in the main buildings of the deserted palm oil plantation. It was a shrewd move by Kallay to put the creek between the hostages and any friendly forces that might approach over land. To the east and west of Gberi Bana were areas of marshland that restricted access to the village from the right bank of Rokel Creek.

In London and Freetown, Foreign Office and Ministry of Defence (MoD) staff tried to assess what had happened. Initially the Whitehall ministries were optimistic. They reported that the men had gone missing in the Masiaka-Forodugu area about 62 miles (100 km) east of the capital, Freetown. They confirmed that they were safe and well, but not free to leave.

---

2 Though obsolete the Soviet-era ZPU-2 anti-aircraft gun remains a formidable weapon that fires a variety of ammunition including armor piercing API (BS.41), API-T (BZT) and I-T (ZP) projectiles. Each barrel has a maximum rate of fire of around 600 rounds per minute, though this is practically limited to about 150 rounds per minute. The AP rounds can penetrate 1.25 inches (32mm) of vertical armor plate at 1,640 feet (500m.)

INITIAL STRATEGY

Once it became clear where the Royal Irish patrol was being held, and by whom, the first priority was to ensure that they were safe and to try to negotiate their release. The West Side Boys were hostile and suspicious and would, therefore, only meet the negotiators at the end of the track from Magbeni.

The face-to-face negotiations that followed were headed by Lt. Col. Simon Fordham, the CO 1 Royal Irish, a shrewd and very experienced officer. He would bring a small team with him for his meetings, while the West Side Boys would arrive fully armed and in large numbers. From the first meeting Lt. Col. Fordham realized that in Kallay he was dealing with "a psychotic, a psychopath who didn't realize the seriousness of what was going on around him." For the West Side Boys the experience of negotiating with a colonel in the British Army was both exhilarating and flattering. They were not to know that each of these meetings helped to build up the intelligence picture of their capabilities and strength.

The Royal Irish RSM who accompanied the colonel on one of these meetings watched a 17-year-old girl soldier put down her RPG7 antitank rocket launcher and walk forward to the Royal Irish Land Rovers, stop, turn around and walk back, pacing out the range. When she reached her RPG7 she adjusted the sights to the correct range and settled down with the launcher on her shoulder to cover the British vehicles.

Unseen down the track behind Lt. Col. Fordham were two officers from the Metropolitan Police Hostage and Crisis Negotiation Unit. They advised the colonel on strategy and briefed and debriefed him before and after the meetings. Since the operation some soldiers have said that they felt the low-key negotiating style convinced the West Side Boys that they were dealing with weak people whom they could bully. They assert that if the negotiating team had arrived in strength with armed men and vehicles it would have given them the authority of overt power and could have ended the crisis.

Ideally if the negotiations had succeeded, the standoff would have been resolved and the patrol released, meaning there would have been no need for the "direct

AUGUST 27, 2000

Negotiations begin for the release of the hostages.

Royal Air Force and Royal Navy helicopters operating at Lungi Airport, Freetown, during Operation *Palliser*. A RAF HC2 Chinook from No 7 Squadron RAF Odiham prepares to take off as a Royal Navy Sea King flies past. (IWM UKLC-2000-049-001-016)

action" of an attack to release the hostages. However, preliminary plans for an attack were already being made. What was needed and would be acquired, through human and electronic intelligence, was detailed information about the West Side Boys and their positions in the villages.

At a meeting on August 27, the West Side Boys demanded the release from detention of Foday Sankoh, who they referred to as "General Papa," along with food and medicine, in exchange for the British troops.

Proof of life

Two days later at the request of Lt. Col. Fordham the two captive officers were allowed to leave the jungle camp accompanied by Kallay to meet the colonel and the hostage negotiating team. This was a "proof of life" meeting to demonstrate that the hostages were still alive. For the benefit of the West Side Boys the captives assured the colonel that the Royal Irish were being treated well, and that no one was injured. To Fordham they looked "the worse for wear." The captain saluted and then held out his hand to the colonel. As their hands closed Lt. Col. Fordham felt the hard shape of a small object that was being "palmed" to him. Only when they withdrew out of sight of the West Side Boys did he open his right hand to see that he held a plastic ball point pen top. In it was a slip of carefully rolled paper.

It was a detailed map of Gberi Bana showing which huts held the hostages, which ones were used by the West Side Boys for accommodation and the possible approach routes to the camp. What was emerging was that Magbeni was the "barracks" for the West Side Boys foot soldiers while Gberi Bana was the "HQ" in which Kallay and his unstable gang leaders were based and where the hostages were held.

The situation seemed to be improving when two days later on the evening of August 31 five of the 11 British soldiers were released, in exchange for a satellite phone and medical supplies. Initially, it was proposed that married men should be released, but at the last moment the West Side Boys decided to keep the RSO and his signals corporal. This allowed two other men to go free—the Royal Irish hostages drew lots for the two tickets to freedom. The RSO was about to make the draw when Sgt. Smith stepped forward and said "Take my name out. I'll stay. We'll let a youngster go."

The other soldiers, the officers and NCOs, would not be released, it was explained to the hostage negotiation team, until the other demands of the West Side Boys had

Soldiers of 1 Para with a Pinzgauer light vehicle in discussion outside a medical tent at Lungi Airport, Freetown, during Operation *Palliser*. (IWM UKLC-2000-049-002-019)

been met. However, the Rangers who had been released were an invaluable intelligence asset in a position to fill in the gaps in the picture that was shaping up.

Lt. Cdr. Tony Cramp RN, the MoD spokesman in Sierra Leone, told the media that the freed soldiers were "in very good condition" and on their way to Freetown. He added, "They are being looked after and they are in close contact with their families and are concerned for their colleagues. They are relaxing and calming down after what happened."

The five freed Royal Irish soldiers were flown to the RFA *Sir Percivale* in Freetown for a detailed debriefing where they would explain how their convoy was captured and where the remaining members of the group were being held.

They described how Kallay had visited the group every day, repeatedly demanding to know why they had driven to his camp. He shouted at them "Explain your mission or I will shoot you."

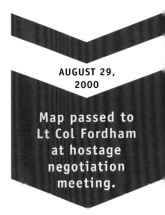

AUGUST 29, 2000

Map passed to Lt Col Fordham at hostage negotiation meeting.

Mock executions

According to the West Side Boys' leader's chief bodyguard "Corporal Blood," several days after the capture Kallay, perhaps drunk or in a drug-induced paranoid low, appeared to have decided he had had enough. Six soldiers were marched to an execution area and bodyguards lined up, stone-faced, pointed their AK47 assault rifles at the captives, and awaited the order to fire.

As the rest of the Britons fell silent, Marshall reasoned with Kallay, who was shouting "I will kill you! I will kill you!"

"He was very cool," said Corporal Blood. "He told Kallay, 'We just came to see you, to tell you to forget fighting. We did not come with any bad intentions. If you kill us, it will not be for any reason.'"

The threats continued for half an hour and then Kallay relented and ordered the men back to their hut in the main camp. It would prove to be one of several mock executions, which were seen by many of the West Side Boys as a form of entertainment.

The West Side Boys were beginning to enjoy their new notoriety and found it exhilarating to be able to make demands that the British negotiators were obliged to fulfil. It was little wonder that the youthful, aggressive and intoxicated young men had affected exotic names and high ranks like "Colonel Savage" and "Colonel Terminator," while their spokesman in dealings with the British styled himself "Colonel Cambodia."

For the British negotiating team in Sierra Leone the drink and drug habits of the West Side Boys made them particularly difficult to work with. Excessive use of cannabis produces short-term memory loss as well as mild paranoia. Agreements that had been concluded one day would have been forgotten within 24 hours. If cocaine was being used by the West Side Boys its aftereffects could make them even more paranoid and forgetful.

The West Side Boys described the hostages as "very comfortable" but British staff in Freetown now knew that Marshall, at this time unnamed in media reports, had been beaten by his captors. It would later emerge that the Sierra Leone Army Liaison Officer (LO) had suffered an even more severe assault. The West Side Boys saw this brave young man, a soldier in the newly structured SLA with a passion for learning and self improvement, as a "traitor." It was a grim fact that Musa Bangura was the "whipping boy" for the patrol suffering greater punishment than the British soldiers. However, a desire to keep the emotional temperature in the negotiations as low as possible was probably the reason that the abuse suffered by the soldiers was not released to the UK media.

Foreigners living in Freetown, including Nigerians and Lebanese, wait to board the helicopters, which will evacuate them from Freetown to Lungi airport during Operation *Palliser*. (IWM UKLC-2000-049-004-003)

Soon after he had received the satellite phone Colonel Cambodia realized that he had a wider audience than that of a military radio net so he called up the BBC African Service. He said the hostages were taken in order to get Britain to pressure President Kabbah to recognize the West Side Boys as a legitimate group, to free their arrested leaders from prison, and to form a new government with seats for their leaders.

The "Colonel" explained that the group had now fallen out with "JP" (Johnny Paul Koroma), who had expressed support for Kabbah. He said they distrusted the government, and would not disarm until their demands were met.

> We won't give up until we revisit the Lomé Peace Accord. That is the first one, and then secondly, they have to release all the AFRC detainees including our wives, our children, and our brothers. Only we need an interim government. In fact the AFRC has got a new leader. No more J.P. because J.P. betrayed us. Now we have got another AFRC representative or a leader here, who is Brigadier-General F. Kallay.

In a rambling interview he explained,

> We are holding on to them so that we'll be able to pass our requests through them to the government because the government is a government against the West Side Boys. We will hold onto them until our demands are solved.

Asked by the BBC African Service how the West Side Boys came to capture the soldiers, Colonel Cambodia replied grandly, "We captured these soldiers because they entered into our area of responsibility without communicating with us or our commanders."

The West Side Boys would soon exhaust the batteries in the satellite phone, but as Richard Connaughton notes in the specialist publication *Small Wars & Insurgencies*,

"This telephone might have proved his [Kallay's] Trojan horse because, through the process of signal interception, the precise location of the bandits could be verified." Electronic warfare specialists from the Royal Corps of Signals and possibly GCHQ Cheltenham not only located the position of the telephone, but after the broadcast to the BBC were able to switch it on and off remotely.

As part of the negotiations Koroma wrote twice to the West Side Boys sending letters via the local Jordanian UNAMSIL troops. In his second letter he urged the gang to release the soldiers:

> The continuing holding of people coming to Sierra Leone to assist in the peace process does not augur well. I therefore ask you that, as in the earlier the better, you free the British soldiers.

As the contacts continued between Lt. Col. Fordham and Kallay, Sierra Leone's Minister of Information, the tough but bookish Dr. Julius Spencer, stated that the government "would not bow to this kind of pressure" by meeting the captors' demands. Now in Freetown the local population looked away or at the ground as British Army Land Rovers drove by. The West Side Boys had humiliated the British Army, the one force that the Sierra Leoneans had hoped would bring stability and security to the country.

A British soldier offers water to a family who are waiting for evacuation during Operation *Palliser*.
(IWM UKLC-2000-049-004-009)

"Delicate and volatile"

On Thursday August 30 British officials in London insisted that negotiations were still the best course. However, they described the situation as becoming "delicate" and "volatile."

Life for the hostages in Gberi Bana was terrifying, humiliating and unpredictable Sometimes the West Side Boys would be friendly and then their mood would change.

The threat to Sierra Leone came from insurgents of all ages—here a child soldier smiles cheerfully for the camera. He has an ex-British Army SLR with a bundle of magazines taped together. While this ensures plenty of ammunition to handle makes the weapon very unbalanced. (Corbis)

One of them regularly pointed guns at the soldiers and threatened to kill them if a rescue bid were mounted.

According to a Sierra Leonean captive, the sadistic camp commandant, the self-styled "Lt. Col." Contobie, demanded that the captives line up, then bow down in front of him and say, "Good morning, Commandant." He boasted that the British had bowed before only three black men: Idi Amin, Chief Bureh (a Sierra Leone leader who had opposed the British rule in the mid-19th century) and now him.

Marshall had to ask permission for his men to eat and be given drinking water. In turn the West Side Boys ordered him to clean the wounds of injured militiamen using cheap local gin as an antiseptic. The major and captain were forced to train 30 male hostages in a parade ground drill on the dirt football field to the north of the village using wooden sticks in place of rifles. The West Side Boys intended to use the abducted men as fighters. However, the West Side Boys did not realize these drill sessions would allow the officers to get to know their fellow captives and identify them after the raid was over.

Meanwhile, in London the MoD was still unable to explain why the Royal Irish had turned off the main road so far from the BTC. The ministry stated that they were surprised the soldiers had disappeared into the bush—but they were not surprised that the men had lunched with Jordanian UN peacekeepers before the journey that led to their capture.

Gen. Mohamed Garba, the Nigerian commander of UNAMSIL, responded that the soldiers had failed to tell the UN about their activities and he disputed the British account of the kidnapping. He agreed that the soldiers from the Royal Irish Regiment were captured while deep inside militia-held jungle, but denied they had met the Jordanian troops.

Around this time, two 22 SAS negotiators were reported to have joined Lt. Col. Fordham's team. One of them was a 34-year-old sergeant who was also tasked with reconnaissance and intelligence gathering. In the guise of a Royal Irish major, he joined in the difficult negotiating process.

According to the popular British newspaper the *Mail on Sunday* a senior military source said, "This sergeant is one of the top soldiers in the world. His record is astonishing. He joined the SAS from the Royal Engineers in 1990 and he is now a key member of A Squadron." In all, the sergeant would make five visits during the negotiations near Gberi Bana.

On his sixth visit to Magbeni, the SAS sergeant, armed with only a Browning 9mm pistol, joined what were in effect last-ditch negotiations. It was at this meeting that a West Side Boy who styled himself Colonel GS (General Staff) announced, "Tell your friends that if I see you again I will cut off your head and eat you. Tell them!"

The sergeant replied, "I'll bear that in mind," to which the GS with a sense of the dramatic shouted back, "No if we meet again one of us must die!"

HMS Argyll's Medical Officer, Surgeon Lt. Jon Carty, had come ashore to join the negotiating team to treat the hostages, should they be released, and if in the volatile atmosphere the situation deteriorated to provide primary casualty care. He recalled, "I was obviously very excited to be given the opportunity to put my training to use, but I soon realized how challenging this was going to be."

1 Para carry out a vehicle patrol in the bush of Sierra Leone during Operation *Palliser*. Though there might be a threat from small arms fire in Sierra Leone there were no mines or IEDs. (IWM UKLC-2000-049-006-003)

The Occra hills, the area where the hostages were held, had been surrounded at a distance by the UNAMSIL forces to prevent the West Side Boys moving the captives. However, the press reported ominously that military sources considered a raid would not be easy given the terrain and the gang's knowledge of the area.

Pressed about the possibility of direct action Lt. Cdr. Tony Cramp said only that the Army was "planning for every contingency." The British media noted that as well as the STTT staff there had been an unspecified number of SAS soldiers in Sierra Leone before the hostage crisis developed.

After Operation *Barras*, the British Army magazine *Soldier* would report that, "In Sierra Leone and in Northwood media operations officers asked reporters not to speculate about a rescue mission. For the sake of giving someone in Britain an interesting read over their cornflakes and toast, the hostages could have died."

As part of the negotiations relatives of the West Side Boys made two visits to the riverside base saying that they wanted to bring both the West Side Boys and the hostages back to Freetown. The first, on August 30, coincided with the release of five hostages and the delivery of the satellite phone. The delegation of relatives offered the West Side Boys bread, sugar and powdered milk, but no money. In a country as impoverished as Sierra Leone these gifts were a very generous and significant gesture.

"They assured us that they will soon come out of the bush after they release the remaining British hostages," said one relative. She added that the fighters wanted Britain and the Freetown government to guarantee immunity from arrest for the gang if they did this.

One mother, Juliet Sesay, said they appealed to their sons saying that the British were in Sierra Leone to help the country. The West Side Boys responded that they had nothing against the British but that the abductions had finally brought attention to their demands, little realizing how unrealistic they were.

AUGUST 31, 2000

Five Rangers released in exchange for satellite phone.

Safe passage

One of the demands of The West Side Boys was for Britain to guarantee them safe passage out of Sierra Leone and to provide them with an education abroad.

The scheme was put to British officials by Koroma after the relatives returned from a visit to Gberi Bana. "Some of them want to get out of the country," he said.

> They want to study in some vocational institute so that when they come back later they will be useful to the country … I think the bottom line is fear. We will talk to the British, we will talk to the government, to guarantee their security.

The West Side Boys wanted those fighters who were not sent abroad to be guaranteed places in Sierra Leone's Army, now in training by the British STTT.

British officials declined to comment while negotiations continued but the proposals seemed to indicate that the West Side Boys had backed away from their original demand for the release of their leaders and other comrades from prison and were seeking a way out of the hostage crisis.

Kallay told relatives he feared that if he freed the British captives his fighters would be vulnerable to attack by the SLA or UN forces. His elder brother, Maxim Sesay, said the leader was seeking assurances from the British for his security, while the West Side Boys were looking for international recognition and also security.

> I wasn't able to see him but I was able to send a message to him with a West Side Boy and I told him he should release the British soldiers … In his answer to me he told me he has no confidence in the government and he wants international recognition, that is

Two Nigerian soldiers serving with the United Nations contingent check the identity card of a local civilian beside a road sign marking the way to Lungi Airport and the airport hotel, Freetown. (IWM UKLC-2000-049-003-012)

A British military vehicle is parked in front of the main entrance to the terminal building of Lungi Airport, Freetown. (IWM UKLC-2000-049-003-023)

why he took them. They were taken so the British government would come to their rescue and he would get international recognition.

He added that the authorities had arrested some of the West Side Boys and that "[Kallay] himself is afraid because of what he has done." Sesay said his brother told him the hostages would be released, "but with conditions."

In an attempt to reassure the hostage takers, Sierra Leone's Attorney General stated he had no plans to prosecute them for holding the soldiers captive. However, in rumor-filled Freetown it was said that the government was split on the issue.

In London, Tony Blair and Foreign Secretary Robin Cook were directly involved, discussing the problem with Gen. Sir Charles Guthrie, Chief of the Defence Staff (CDS), at a Cabinet Committee meeting.

In Sierra Leone, Lt. Cdr. Tony Cramp announced:

> There were further meetings yesterday and it is felt that things are moving forward ... Things are still positive and we remain confident of getting them out through dialogue and talking. We are moving forward. We are not complacent about it but we are still confident.

A British Army Lynx helicopter is prepared for a mission at Lungi Airport, Freetown, during Operation *Palliser*. Army Air Corps' Lynx attack helicopters would play a critical role in Operation *Barras*. (IWM UKLC-2000-049-003-024)

As the pressure increased Surgeon Lt. Carty was relocated to RFA *Sir Percivale* to act as triage officer. In an interview in the Navy News, he recalled:

> My role changed along with the emphasis of the operation. I was told that within the next 48 to 72 hours an operation to extract the hostages would be initiated. Since the resultant casualties would be treated on *Sir Percivale*, I was moved there to assist with medical support.

Though air traffic at Lungi airport had increased dramatically HMS *Argyll*'s Lynx helicopter was still the only UK aircraft available, and was consequently in demand for everything from passenger transfers to movement of stores.

However, given the increased threat to British forces, Cpl. Nick Tryon from *Argyll*'s Royal Marines detachment was embarked to "ride shotgun" for the aircraft and crew. The pilot, Lt. Cdr. Jones, said, "I was very pleased to have Cpl. Tryon on board, particularly in such a potentially hostile operational environment."

Now not only was *Argyll*'s Lynx still operating in a variety of supporting roles—reconnaissance, casualty evacuation, transfer of personnel—but *Argyll*'s flight deck was also used as a temporary overnight base for two Army Mk 7 Lynx AH helicopters. They had arrived in Freetown aboard an RAF C130 Hercules and, having been assembled at Lungi airport, were flown directly to the ship.

PLAN

On August 30, a signal was received at the HQ of 1 Para at Connaught Barracks in Dover, Kent. They were to ring the Director Special Forces (DSF). At the same time Capt. Liam Cradden, the Operations Officer, had been informed that there was a drama in Sierra Leone and 1 Para might be involved. The requirement was for a company group to support Special Forces and to be ready to move as soon as possible.

At the time the battalion was on no formal notice to move; it had been moved out of 16 Air Assault Brigade, the balanced force designed for rapid intervention using fixed wing and helicopter assets, and was now "out of role" and in 2 South East Brigade, a regional brigade. The Battalion, therefore, had no operational role except for a Northern Ireland tour scheduled at the end of the year. Many officers were still unpacking kit and possessions following the move from Aldershot.

A Coy, commanded by Maj. Matthew Lowe, was selected by the shrewd and experienced 1 Para CO because he knew it was jungle trained, with experience in field firing during Exercise *Red Stripe* in Jamaica, and had NCOs who had been on Operation *Palliser*.

When Maj. Lowe attended his first briefing at Joint Task Force Head Quarters (JTFHQ) he learned that he would be required to assemble a force of between 120 and 140 men. Their mission was still undefined but would be part of the hostage rescue operation. What they would be required to do within this operation was still being addressed by the JTFHQ. In fact at this stage the Special Forces planning group had no defined role for the company group but knew that the numbers and fire power might be useful.

Maj Lowe worked out a Force Element Table (FET) that consisted of the basic Coy HQ and three Rifle Platoons who would carry two L7A2 7.62 mm General Purpose Machine Guns (GPMGs) per section. Though the 25.6-pound (11.65 kg) GPMG is a heavier weapon than the magazine-fed Light Support Weapon (LSW) Maj. Lowe felt that the ability of the belt-fed GPMG to deliver sustained fire made it better for the action that he anticipated the company would be fighting.[3]

According to its commander, the company was receiving "a reassuringly large amount of ammunition … each platoon holding roughly 6,500 rounds of 5.56 Ball, 6000 rounds of 7.62 mm 4Bit, 170 Grenades (L2 HE and Red Phosphorus smoke) and 50 bombs for the 51mm mortar."

The company group was configured to give Maj. Lowe the fire-power to "Find and Fix" the enemy, in other words to tie down the West Side Boys and neutralize them while the SAS extracted the hostages. Though Maj. Lowe would receive specialist units from within 1 Para to reinforce A Coy he did not "cherry pick" individual soldiers from other companies within the battalion because as a company the men knew each other. They were already configured in a Northern Ireland Orbat and in the boyish Capt Danny Matthews

Military stores and vehicles parked on the apron at Lungi Airport, Freetown, after being unloaded from an Antonov cargo aircraft. (IWM UKLC-2000-049-003-028)

---

3 The GPMG has a cyclic rate of fire of between 650 and 1,000 rounds a minute so a platoon with one gun per section would be capable of delivering between 3,900 and 6,000 rounds a minute onto a target.

had a very experienced second-in-command. Within A Coy were ten new recruits, two weeks out of the Infantry Training Centre (ITC) at Catterick in Yorkshire. They were retained on the grounds that, as a senior officer put it, "if you're good enough to join the Battalion you're good enough to go on ops...."

Extra talent

An important reason why the CO did not try to "pack" A Coy with extra talent was that this would destroy the coherence of other companies and even the Battalion and they might later be required to deploy to Sierra Leone as reinforcements. As a result, Maj. Lowe was in command of a very young company with an average age of 19. The young men of A Coy would be up against an armed gang made up of men and women of roughly the same average age. However, that was the only thing they had in common. The West Side Boys might be ill-trained and undisciplined but, as one veteran remarked afterwards, the British knew that they would stand and fight.

As the A Company Group was formed sub-units and formations from within the battalion were attached. They might not all be deployed in the initial attack but could be flown in to reinforce the company when it was on the ground. Many of them were *Palliser* veterans. The CO reasoned that if the new operation in Sierra Leone needed to be expanded the infrastructure would be in place to support a second company or even the battalion.

The assets attached to A Coy included the Patrols Platoon, which comprised the HQ and three patrols—a Signals Group consisting of the main station, a tactical one on foot and the LO's radios who would be in contact with the Special Forces and helicopters. Accurate long-range fire would be delivered by two sniper pairs equipped with the L115A1 Long Range Rifle. There would be four three-man HMG sections with the Browning .5-in. (12.7 mm) machine gun mounted on WMIKs. The Mortar Section, with its HQ and three 3.2-in. (81mm) L16 mortars with a maximum range of 19,028 ft. (5,800 m) firing High Explosive (HE) bombs, would give the company effective indirect fire. The Regimental Medical Officer (RMO), Capt. Reece Thomas, was attached to the expanded Company Aid Post so that it was virtually the Regimental Aid Post and, finally, there was the vital Echelon Element commanded by the Technical Quartermaster (QM(T)), Pete Lodge.

The ammunition for the company group was ordered on the same day that the FET was drawn up. Since there would be no threat from armored vehicles the company would only carry the 2.6-inch (66 mm) LAW—an antitank weapon that though obsolescent would be very effective against buildings and bunkers.[4] Some soldiers were equipped with the Rifle Grenade General Service (RGGS) while others would carry slung across their shoulders the compact haversacks containing the M18 A1 Claymore directional antipersonnel (AP) mines. The mines would be used to secure the perimeter against West Side Boy counterattacks once the village had been cleared.

On Thursday August 31 a prepared cover story was issued that the company was on standby to reinforce the UK Spearhead battalion, the 1st Battalion The Grenadier Guards, a force held in readiness for quick-reaction operations. The company would move to South Cerney in Wiltshire to be ready for a "Readiness to Move" exercise with the Guards.

---

4 The 2.6-inch (66 mm) Light antitank weapon (LAW) is still part of the armory of the elite Parachute Regiment Pathfinders and A Coy had veterans of the Pathfinders who would know how effective the compact weapon was. It would also be used by D Squadron in their operations. The LAW is a US-designed, one-shot, disposable, telescopic weapon that weighs only 6 pounds (3.45 kg) and is 29.7 inches (775 mm) long when telescoped down. It can penetrate around 300millimeters of armour and has an effective range of 722 feet (220 m.)

After the operation was over some commentators asked why the Guards had not been employed to support D Squadron. However, the Parachute Regiment is the closest that the British Army has to "shock troops." Many men who have passed "P Company," the gruelling tests of courage and stamina to enter "Para Reg," have gone on to face the even tougher challenge of Selection for the SAS. At the outset of the operation the men from A Coy found that they had a number of old friends in D Squadron, which reinforced the bond.

It may have been that it was the DSF who pressed for the use of "Para Reg." The Parachute Regiment had exercised with "The Regiment," as the SAS is known colloquially, and had been used as backup for Special Forces (SF) in other operations. They were consistently well trained and motivated and had experience in air assault operations.

One airborne veteran commented:

> To be fair, you cannot have an organization that carries out an additional level of selection to the rest of the infantry and one that specializes in light, airborne and heliborne operations and then pretend it is the same as the line infantry. *Barras* was tailor made for a Para Coy.

Operational security

To ensure that there was no accidental breach of security all mobile phones were collected before Maj. Lowe addressed his company at the Operational Mounting Centre (OMC) at South Cerney, Gloucestershire.

There was the silence of total concentration in the hangar when he explained that they were not on exercise, this was an operational deployment.

The initial briefing for A Company Group's part in the rescue mission was held in the suite of contingency planning offices adjoining one of the hangars at the OMC. The 1 Para Intelligence Officer had come directly from the Permanent Joint Head Quarters (PJHQ) at Northwood and described the ground and what was known of the enemy.

Maj. Lowe had identified a planning group that consisted of himself, the three platoon commanders, operations officer (G3), intelligence team (G2), a clerk and a signaller. He had with him a folder that listed all elements of the company group, which he recalled would "prove invaluable."

The Ops Officer Capt. Cradden and the Intelligence Officer (IO) Capt. Adam Jowett working through the night had produced an aide-mémoire. Issued to all the men at the OMC, it contained the low-level lessons that had been learned by the battalion during Operation *Palliser*. This included basic administration and advice

D Squadron 22 SAS

1 Trooper D Squadron 22 SAS. While this figure is conjectural it is based on the theory that, to ensure a low profile, the SAS would adopt kit and clothing similar to that of the men of A Coy 1 Para. The trooper has the paratrooper's helmet, combat body armor and tropical DPM uniform. **2** Diemaco C7A1 .2-inch (5.56 mm) Assault Rifle with M203 1.6-inch (40 mm) grenade launcher. The 30-round magazine on the rifle can also be fitted to the FN Minimi light machine gun. **3** PLCE day pack – this would be used to carry Passive Night Goggles, 24 hour ration pack, extra ammunition, explosives and demolition equipment. **4** Directional amplified microphone—this system was manufactured for the civilian market and can be folded down for stowage. **5** The Commando version of the FN .21-inch (5.56mm) Minimi light machine gun with telescopic butt, short barrel, and plastic ammunition box holding 200 rounds

As part of an exercise in reassuring the local population, during a pause in a patrol, three soldiers from 1 Para confer under the regimental flag taken with them into the bush of Sierra Leone. (IWM UKLC-2000-049-006-019)

about hydration as well as background information about the country and people of Sierra Leone. In quiet moments at South Cerney the "Toms" stretched out and leafed through the aide-mémoire.

CSM Chiswell had also worked through the night breaking down the stores and distributing them to the soldiers. At this stage it was not known how much time and space the company would have for battle preparations once it arrived in Africa. The soldiers had already updated their inoculations, been issued with antimalaria tablets (Lariam) and prepared their equipment for a jungle deployment. Next of Kin Forms, which gave details of the close relative who was to be contacted if the soldier became a casualty, were updated. Normally this was a wife, sibling or parent. The two identity discs on their metal chains were checked against the soldier's name, blood group, religion and service number. The company group, backed by all the resources that the battalion could provide, was resolved and focused.

The planning group flew to Dakar on Sunday morning. Here, the intelligence that had been gathered by SAS patrols who had been operating around the West Side Boys' bases was studied along with maps and photographs.

By September 5, the SAS had two patrols on the ground. They had been inserted from Rokel Creek by assault boats handled expertly by an SBS coxswain. The patrols, in position on either side of the creek, remained hidden by day and at night infiltrated through the thick bush to monitor the movements around the West Side Boys' bases, identify weapons and log the routine in the two camps either side of the creek. They were also tasked with identifying viable helicopter landing zones.

The village of Magbeni, covered by an SAS observation team call sign SGA (Sierra Green Alpha), was identified as the objective for the 1 Para company group. On the map it consisted of 29 buildings ranged along a track that ran parallel to Rokel Creek. Since the inhabitants had been driven out by the West Side Boys many of the buildings had collapsed and the jungle had encroached on the little vegetable gardens. Some of the more substantial buildings were still standing and could be used to mount an effective defense. The jungle vegetation including 6.5-foot (2m) high elephant grass grew close to the central track and, like some of the buildings, offered cover for both the Paras and their adversaries. For planning the buildings were identified by the letters from the phonetic alphabet from T (Tango) to Z (Zulu) and the platoons tasked with clusters of buildings as their objective.

A steady stream of high-grade intelligence was coming in from SAS observation teams, including information that some buildings held civilians, which meant that the plan had to be modified and updated. A Restricted Fire Line was established so that the company would advance safely supported by direct and indirect fire.

The major threat to any attack was the HMG in the village, which could engage helicopters landing near the village or across the river at Gberi Bana. However the HMG position was screened by buildings and jungle vegetation so it was decided that it would need to be destroyed by the Army Air Corps Lynx attack helicopters at the start of the operation using its pintle-mounted machine gun. The plan called for the Lynx crew, using night vision goggles, to operate at low level hitting targets such as the armed vehicles that were a potential threat to the Paras. The attack helicopters

would engage any craft that attempted to cross Rokel Creek and any people who appeared on the banks, since friendly forces would not be in this area.

At some stage in the planning process Maj. Lowe was given the mission "to defeat" the forces in the village. This was significant, because had the company been told they were "to destroy" the West Side Boys in Magbeni then the gang would have suffered heavier casualties since fewer would have been given the opportunity to run away or hide.

There were three options for insertion available to both D Squadron and A Coy. The Paras looked at an approach over land using vehicles like WMIK, Pinzgauer Turbo D (4 x 4) trucks or even, it was suggested, quad bikes. However, there was only one track into the village and this was covered by West Side Boys' road blocks that would at least delay the attack and this would put the hostages at risk. Rokel Creek, which had been used to insert the two observation teams, was considered. However, the sand banks and currents were a hazard. Three CH47 Chinooks of the RAF Joint Special Forces Aviation Wing were in country with very experienced crews and as the mission became clearer, an air assault though inherently risky seemed the best and most reliable option. The Chinooks had deployed to the theater during Operation *Palliser* and had played a significant role in operations in support of isolated UNAMSIL detachments under attack by the RUF.

A paratrooper from 1 Para patrols Lungi Airport, Freetown. In the background are two of the four Royal Air Force HC2 Chinook helicopters of No 7 Squadron RAF. Chinooks from the RAF Special Forces Squadron would be used to insert troops during Operation *Barras*. (IWM UKLC-2000-049-006-025)

Rescue plans

Two rescue plans had been developed—one was a deliberate operation and the other an emergency action plan. The deliberate operation would see troops moving covertly to the fringes of the camp and, at dawn, slip in to release the hostages before the West Side Boys were awake and alert. A distraction would then be arranged that would allow the rescuers to overpower the West Side Boys and release the Sierra Leonean hostages. However, as the Paras realized, the terrain, jungle and West Side Boys' road blocks made a stealthy overland approach virtually impossible.

The planning team at SAS Group HQ at Regents Park Barracks, London (known simply as "Group") opted for an enhanced emergency action plan—it would be "enhanced" because D Squadron and A Coy would be able to choose the time of the assault.

Despite strict operational security within the A Company Group and Battalion the possibility that a rescue operation might be mounted had already filtered out to the public. HQ LAND Command had been designated the supporting headquarters. In the words of one officer, "it started sending signals all over the place (many of them totally unnecessary) and so from the outset the deployment of the Paras was in the public domain." Signals went to other Spearhead units about the upcoming operation that even identified the size of the formation and its role in a hostage rescue operation.

Whether this information was leaked by accident, or released deliberately as part of a negotiating ploy to be fed into the Freetown rumor mill, is hard to say but soon the British papers were carrying stories mentioning The Parachute Regiment and Sierra Leone. On Tuesday September 5 *The Guardian* newspaper ran the headline "Paratroopers fly to West Africa as 'contingency.'" A day later the press in Freetown reported that British paratroopers had arrived in Freetown, even as negotiators continued talks with the West Side Boys.

If the story were intended to be a piece of psychological warfare it did not appear to have been successful. If the West Side Boys had heard of the 1 Para deployment to Sierra Leone, their arrogant manner during the negotiations indicated that this fact did not impress or unduly concern them.

In Freetown, when asked about the deployment of the Paras, Lt. Cdr. Tony Cramp said:

> This is no way signifies any imminent military action in Sierra Leone. It is just a sensible contingency measure to place troops in the region. We have not ruled out any options for releasing the captives. But the talks are making progress and we are hopeful that this can be ended peacefully.

However, for the Special Forces the reports that the Paras were destined for Sierra Leone were a useful cover for their deployment.

Soldiers from 1 Para sort ration packs in their camp amongst the trees in Sierra Leone. Local poverty shocked soldiers who would see their discarded food containers quickly recycled to carry water or be used as storage. (IWM UKLC-2000-049-006-027)

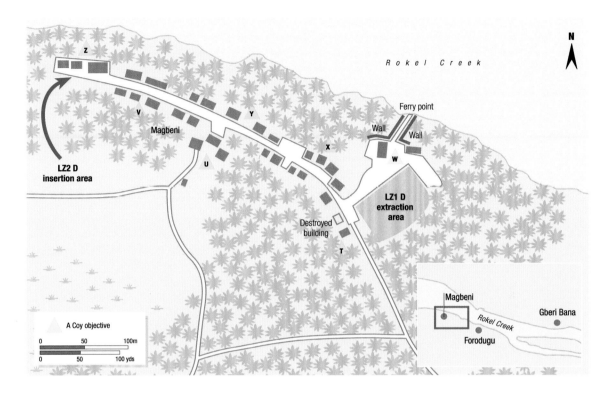

The village of Magbeni.

The 130 men of the A Company Group, concentrating on platoon and company live firing and training, were isolated from these reports in their camp near Hastings, a village with an airstrip at the foot of the Peninsula Mountains. D Squadron had already set up their base at Camp Hastings and many of the men from A Coy recognized old friends who had served in Paras before passing Selection and joining the SAS. Cpl. David Aitchinson of 1 Para remembered D Squadron as supremely professional but also a "laid back chilled organization." Some of the men in D Squadron had grown beards and all wore the anonymous camouflaged jungle hat that in the humid climate of West Africa took on an individual shape and character.

As the media began to speculate about a possible rescue operation the MoD had sent an encrypted signal to the captain of the RFA *Argus* (A 135), which had left British waters to support an exercise off Turkey, ordering him to head straight for Sierra Leone. Two Lynx helicopters were also taken by a C130 Hercules to Dakar and then on to Lungi Airport. The two Lynxes and the RAF Chinooks already in the country would later be deployed to the small airfield at Hastings, about 30 miles (48km) south of Freetown.

The men of A Company Group had not arrived in Sierra Leone as a formed group, but by platoon and sub unit. While this was good for security it meant that now that they were in country at Hastings some units had time to get in more training than others. Section and platoon commanders concentrated on live firing and rehearsing the possible sequences of attack on their objectives. The platoon commanders had laid out an exact scale representation of their objectives in the 656-foot (200m) strip village of Magbeni and walked and talked their soldiers through the attack. Live firing exercises sharpened their tactical skills in an area that, being field firing ranges, daily heard the sound of gunfire. Here as the plan took shape the company rehearsed the attack. It allowed the planning group to establish whether the company should fight through the village in a sequenced phased attack or as a simultaneous assault.

Two possible helicopter Landing Zones (LZ) had been identified for A Coy. One, at the eastern end of the village, measuring about 328 feet (100 m) x 262 feet (80 m), was a rough football pitch close to the ferry point. As an additional navigation reference point for the pilots about 656 feet (200 m) to the south-east were three large trees that stood proud of the jungle canopy. It was designated LZ1.

If the Paras landed at LZ1 they would have the advantage of a shock action since they would be almost on top of the village, but they would be exposed to close-range direct fire. If their mission was to destroy the West Side Boys this site would put them in position to sweep westwards driving the gang into the dead end of the village. However, they would need two Chinook lifts to deliver the company and to launch the attack.

LZ2 to the south-west of Magbeni seemed to be a grassy area with a belt of jungle between it and the village. The reconnaissance by SAS observation team Sierra Green Bravo (SGB) had revealed that it was marshy but it was seen as viable. What clinched the choice was that A Coy would initially have only one Chinook allocated to insert troops. Once these men were on the ground the helicopter would turn around and bring in the balance of the company group—it was going to have to be a sequenced attack launched from LZ2.

The rehearsals in the tropical heat confirmed that the Paras would need to fight carrying the minimum equipment—ammunition, water and first field dressings.

The soldiers would wear helmets and combat body armor (CBA)—though the weight would make them sweat and consequently dehydrate, it was reckoned that the price was worth it since it was hoped that it would still be cool during the pre-dawn attack. Prior to the operation there was considerable debate about whether it should be worn since it was feared that men could become heat casualties, particularly those carrying radios and weapons like the GPMG or the barrel, base plate and trip of the 3.2-inch (81 mm) mortar. The GPMG gunners would probably have 600 rounds of belted ammunition and their No. 2 would carry a further 200 along with rifle and magazines.

The CBA would give protection against .03-ounce (1.10g) fragments travelling at 1.460 feet/second (445m/sec) and hits by rifle fire at longer ranges. In the fighting that would follow, the decision would be more than justified.

The men of D Squadron would be carrying more equipment since there was a chance they would be in action in Gberi Bana for some hours. In their Bergens were

With stability restored by the presence of British forces, the streets of downtown Freetown become busy with traffic and low level commerce. The arrival of the Amphibious Readiness Group and HMS Ocean allowed reconstruction work to be undertaken. (Private Collection)

24 hour ration packs, ammunition, plastic explosives and Passive Night Goggles in case the quick onset of the tropical night caught the men still clearing the village after dark.

At Seaview House, the British military HQ on a hillside above the High Commission in Freetown, the DSF with his small HQ including CO 22 SAS and OC D Squadron had been in place with secure radio links to the observation teams since Thursday September 7. DSF was also in communication upwards to the PJHQ and CBR. It was a tight-knit group working on the basis that plans and intelligence were for UK eyes only.

A year after *Barras* Richard Connaughton wrote that:

> The tactical commander was almost certainly SF (Special Forces) who would have taken a significant number of his regimental officers with him. SF have a strong family bond, trusting only those whom they know and respect. There was an obvious requirement for a quasi-operational level headquarters, probably at Freetown with channels open to PJHQ. Command of this HQ was self-selected.

A critical part of the HQ were the three members of the Tactical Communications Wing, RAF who would coordinate the operations of the attack helicopters and the Chinooks operating in marginal light conditions in a congested air space.

Back at Group, one SAS officer had a strongly personal interest in the operation. Maj. Tim Collins of the Royal Irish had volunteered for the SAS in 1988 and served three tours with 22 SAS. In breaks between his tours with Special Forces he had commanded C Company 1 RIR. The men held captive were very much his friends.

> ... within my heart I didn't expect to see any of the captives again. But we had to try, and there was a lesson to be delivered ... this mission had to discourage the RUF and their kind from interfering with British servicemen when they come calling with their hands extended.

Describing his feelings about the planned operation he recalled that "I put it more succinctly. Make it Bibliscal."

A Marine of 42 Commando, Royal Marines, on sentry duty in the bush of Sierra Leone during Operation *Palliser*. Malaria and dehydration were an added problem along with the Revolutionary United Front. (IWM UKLC-2000-002-007)

THE RAID

The decision to launch the rescue operation was taken on Saturday September 9, after Colonel Cambodia insisted that the West Side Boys would hand over the six remaining British captives only once a new interim government had been formed. Earlier demands by the West Side Boys had been for the negotiators to produce a generator, outboard motors and supplies including cigarettes. The negotiators now decided these were simply delaying tactics. More alarmingly, the SAS team covering the Gberi Bana had seen no sign of life from the building holding the hostages.

Now the UK defense chiefs warned that the rebels' threats to kill the hostages had to be taken seriously—and cited the mock executions. They also feared the West Side Boys might move or split up the group. Kallay said that if his demands were not met he would take the Britons further inland, implicitly suggesting that they would then be handed to the RUF. As one British official put it:

> We were being strung along ... It became clear that Kallay had no intention of releasing the men ... That view was borne out after the raid. The hostages later told us that they were sure they would be executed if we did not rescue them. There was no way they were going to be allowed to walk away.

At Chequers, his official country residence, the British Prime Minister had been updated again on the afternoon of Saturday September 9 and told that the raid would start at first light on Sunday morning. He had already given permission to mount the rescue several days earlier when he was at the UN Millennium Summit in New York, but once again he gave the operation his endorsement. In London the Cabinet Office Briefing Room (COBR) gave the operation the go-ahead.

Final preparations

Known informally as "Cobra," COBR is an ad hoc group formed by the government to handle crises and emergencies and is chaired by a senior minister with junior Defence and Foreign Affairs Ministers and advisers representing the police, MI5, MI6 and the SAS. The public first became aware of its existence during Operation *Nimrod*, the SAS operation to liberate hostages held by Iraqi-backed terrorists in the Iranian Embassy at Princess Gate on May 6, 1980. During *Barras* the DSF would probably have been represented by his Chief of Staff. PJHQ would provide the support, but it would be COBR that would take the final decision whether to launch the operation. Within COBR there was a smaller group, the Cabinet Office Group, chaired by a senior civil servant. Throughout the crisis they had been keen to resolve the situation through negotiation; however, now the time for talking had run out.

In Freetown President Kabbah had already given the JTFHQ carte blanche to conduct an operation against the West Side Boys at a time of their choosing. The major from the Army Legal Corps, who had flown out with the JTFHQ, had brought a document giving the authorization from the Sierra Leonean Police for operation against the West Side Boys. Inspector Keith Biddle, the British head of the Sierra Leone Police Authority, had signed it for the Sierra Leonean Police and now the action against the West Side Boys became a military rather than a police responsibility.

On Saturday September 9, Lt. Col. Fordham was able to make a "proof of life" telephone call to the hostages. That evening the men of A Coy and D Squadron received their final orders for Operation *Barras*.

Now at 0500hrs, in the tropical darkness of Sunday morning, on the airstrip at the Hastings Battle Camp, the young paratroopers of A Coy were formed up in their sticks. As soon as they reached the LZ they would be off the helicopter, racing to be clear of the vulnerable aircraft and to secure the perimeter of the LZ.

For 19-year-old Pte. Julian Sheard who had recently joined the battalion this was a dramatic and challenging introduction to the business of soldiering:

> I did not expect something like this quite so early on. I had not really settled in. I hadn't even got my kit for the jumps course fully sorted out.

However, like the other young Paras in A Coy he would not disappoint the confidence placed in him by his Commanding Officer. Sheard probably summed up the views of everyone in the company:

> You knew it was the real thing from the off and were very worried. You were worried for your own safety of course, but you were more worried about letting the team down.

In the Mk 7 Lynx AH helicopter the crew and gunners using their night vision equipment made a final visual check of their weapons and controls. The troopers from D Squadron checked their weapons and fast roping equipment.

Flying with Passive Night Goggles the pilots of the CH47 Chinook Mk 3 helicopters initially had a green luminescent picture of the jungle visible below them. The GPS position of the LZs had been programed in for an exact touchdown. The close target reconnaissance by SAS patrol call sign SGA of Gberi Bana and SGB of Magbeni had been detailed and thorough.

Not far away from Magbeni on the north side of the river, at the end of a 2.8-mile (4.5 km) track leading from a palm oil plantation was the cluster of huts that made up Gberi Bana. In happier times it was the landing site for the ferry from Magbeni. Among the buildings near the road were five low mud-and-cement buildings. The

SEPTEMBER 9, 2000

Decision taken to launch rescue mission.

Two Marines from 42 Commando, Royal Marines guard the sandbagged entrance to Lungi Airport, Freetown. As the airport was secure on a peninsula and protected by the sea on three sides, many foreign nationals were happy to remain there until Freetown was no longer threatened. (IWM UKLC-2000-049-003-006)

Brigadier David Richards *(left)* commanding British forces in Operation *Palliser* at the morning briefing often known as "Morning Prayers" with military and Foreign Office staff. As general he would command ISAF forces in Afghanistan in 2006 and in so doing be the first British general to have US forces under his command since World War II. (IWM UKLC-2000-049-001-002)

dense vegetation on this side of the creek allowed the six-man SAS patrol call sign SGA to move close to the buildings and identify the substantial structure that was the prison for the British captives and the building next to it that held 22 Sierra Leonean civilians kidnapped a week earlier. The other three buildings were home to Kallay and his senior commanders.

The terrain that made it difficult to reconnoiter and attack also made it an ideal prison. Escape on foot would only be possible to the north but while the scrub might offer cover there were also treacherous fingers of swampy ground running inland from the creek. Lesser men might have thought that escape was virtually impossible and resigned themselves to death. However, the soldiers of the Royal Irish had from the outset begun making plans to escape. They planned to wait until their guards were unconscious in a drug- and drink-induced sleep, break out of their prison, and using empty water containers for flotation swim down Rokel Creek.

The entrance to Lungi Airport, Freetown, guarded by 42 Commando, Royal Marines. The securing of this was a key objective of Operation *Palliser*. Two Nigerian soldiers of the United Nations contingent consult in the foreground while a British vehicle, carrying men from 42 Commando, drives out of Lungi Airport. (IWM UKLC-2000-049-002-034)

SGA had concealed themselves in swamps that were in places less than 820 feet (250 m) from Gberi Bana. However, on the south side of the creek cover was sparse around Magbeni and restricted the operations of the four-man team SGB. For both patrols it would be a test of stamina and character as, surviving on the cold rations and water they had brought into their hides, they endured attacks by the diverse insect life around the river. Liquid and solid human waste, which would smell strongly in the jungle, had to be collected in plastic bags and stowed away to prevent discovery.

Along with men of the Parachute Regiment and Royal Marines, Special Forces also entered Sierra Leone, but maintained a low profile. Here civilian pickups collect men at Lungi Airport, Freetown. The Special Forces helped direct operations against the RUF and ensured there was an SF presence in theater before D Squadron deployed. (Andy Chittock)

BRITISH FORCES INVOLVED IN OPERATION BARRAS

A Coy 1 Para with a core of HQ personnel—130 officers and men

D Squadron 22 SAS—40 officers and troopers, about 20 men short of the full strength of the squadron. This was probably to ensure that two helicopters could make one lift.

Special Forces HQ personnel

Field Surgical Team from 16 Close Support Medical Regiment RAMC

Royal Irish patrol—initially 11 men, six at the time of *Barras*

RFA *Sir Percivale*

RFA *Argus*

HMS *Argyll* plus her Lynx helicopter

7 Squadron Joint Special Forces Aviation Wing—three CH47 Chinook helicopters

657 Squadron Army Air Corps—two Westland Lynx helicopters

Mi-24 gunship as air support

Tactical Communications Wing RAF—three members

A soldier of 2 Royal Anglian lets a local youngster peer through the optical sight of his L85A1 rifle during Operation *Basilica*. *Basilica* was the training program for the Sierra Leone Army that would later be undertaken by men of The Royal Irish. (IWM UKLC-2000-049-006-005)

A soldier of 2 Royal Anglian lets a local youngster peer through the optical sight of his L85A1 rifle during Operation *Basilica*. *Basilica* was the training program for the Sierra Leone Army that would later be undertaken by men of The Royal Irish. (IWM UKLC-2000-049-006-005)

SBU—Small Boys Unit

The patrols were under constant threat of chance discovery by the armed children of the West Side Boys' Small Boys Unit (SBU) who might be roaming the area. Betty Sams, a Sierra Leonean woman who had been held captive for ten days at Magbeni, recalled the terrifying child soldiers of the SBU:

> There were always a lot of them around ... They were used as servants by the bigger members of the West Side Boys and as bodyguards because none of the older members of the group, especially not the leaders, trusted one another.

Mrs Sams remembered a 14-year-old boy known simply as "Killer":

> He was one of the worst. The adults were all scared of him. He was really tiny, he looked like he was 11 or 12, but when he looked at people, they fell silent.

Before their rescue the Royal Irish soldiers were constantly surrounded by child fighters, some as young as ten, from the SBU. One Sierra Leonean captive recalled that "There were more children than adults." "Gangsta rap" music blared from radios and ganja soup—made with marijuana—was part of the daily diet of drugs and drink for the militiamen.

Evading these lethal children, the SAS patrols would use burst transmission and a satellite link to send back the intelligence summaries. To save time and battery life some of this information would have been formatted into Standard Operating Procedures and sent as a simple alphanumeric code. Popular newspapers, television and films are fascinated by the idea of Special Forces soldiers going into action with a dazzling armory of high tech equipment and although the teams may have used portable listening devices to eavesdrop on the conversations in the villages, in reality the two patrols would rely to a large extent on their eyes, ears and even their sense of smell to gather intelligence. In some instances they infiltrated to the edge of the villages by swimming through the muddy waters of Rokel Creek.

The patrols estimated there were about 50 to 100 West Side Boys in each village camp and among the weapons that had been identified were the twin ZPU-2 .57 inch (14.5 mm) that had blocked the Royal Irish patrol. In addition they had 2.4 inch (60 mm) and 3.2 inch (81 mm) mortars, RPGs, Kalashnikovs, medium machine guns and, it was thought, antipersonnel mines and grenades. In Magbeni, besides the captured SLA Bedford 4.48-ton (4-tonne), they had pickup trucks mounting machine guns bolted to the cargo floor that had been dubbed "Technicals" after the name first used by the armed clans in Somalia in the 1990s. The three Royal Irish Land Rovers were also located in the village. These vehicles combined to give the West Side Boys both mobility and considerable firepower.

It was believed that the mortars and machine guns sited in Magbeni covering the approaches from the south would also be able to engage targets in Gberi Bana across Rokel Creek. The position was defended in depth because a West Side Boy battalion controlled Laia Junction to the south of Magbeni. These men could counterattack any forces in Magbeni and would block any overland approach.

It is only possible to surmise about how the 40 men of D Squadron were deployed on the hostage extraction operation. It is probable that it involved one Chinook call sign S1 (Sierra One) carrying the hostage rescue team who would fast rope down while the helicopter hovered at minimum height as close as possible to the buildings housing the hostages. The priority of this team call sign S10 or Sierra One Zero was to secure the hostages and remove them from danger as quickly as possible. They would be backed up by a substantial force of four fire teams with call signs numbering from S20 to S60. Meanwhile, fire teams S70 to S12 would be inserted by the second Chinook call sign S2 to clear the area and kill or capture key West Side Boys leaders.

Fast roping is a technique in which soldiers slide down ropes with only leather gloves to protect their hands and slow their descent. They are then on the ground unencumbered by carabiners or abseiling harness. Just visible through the fronds of the oil palm trees, the Chinooks would present a fleeting target to the West Side Boys. The four-man patrols who were on the ground would simultaneously be engaging the West Side Boys who might attempt to shoot at the helicopter or kill the hostages.

Two insertion points had been identified as LZ1 for Chinook S1 and LZ2 for S2, the former south of Gberi Bana on a clearing outside a house occupied by a West Side Boys leader identified as Calm Down Fresh and the latter north of Gberi Bana outside the building occupied by Colonel Cambodia. The pre-dawn attack made it likely that the West Side Boys would be sleeping and that the hostages would be concentrated in one location.

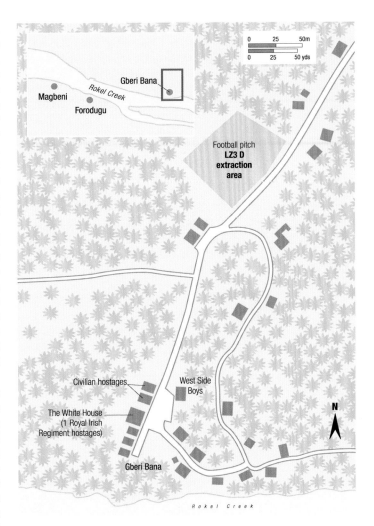

The village of Gberi Bana.

As the hostage rescue team held off the West Side Boys and grabbed the Royal Irish the Chinooks would land on the football pitch/parade ground designated LZ3 about 492 feet (150 m) north of Gberi Bana and the soldiers would be picked up and flown out to *Sir Percivale*. At an early stage in the discussions COBR had been in complete agreement that Cpl. Bangura would be regarded as part of the British group and his evacuation given the same priority as that of the Royal Irish.

SAS—focused violence

While Special Forces conventionally rely on stealth and speed, in *Barras* on both sides of Rokel Creek the Paras and SAS would put in attacks that would be characterized by focused violence. The SAS estimated that they had 60 seconds to complete their rescue mission. After that the shock of the assault would be over and the West Side Boys could be expected to fight back.

An advantage for the SAS team would be that the officers and NCOs in the Royal Irish would be a disciplined group, quick to respond to orders and instructions. The unknown factor would be the reactions of the Sierra Leonean captives and also whether the West Side Boys would attempt to hide amongst them. As a precaution everyone who was alive, except the recognizable British soldiers, would be secured with handcuffs before they were flown out. They would then be delivered to the JordBat location where West Side Boys could be identified and separated from the hostages. In the event the West Side Boys had shaved the heads of their male captives, which made identification quick and easy.

The planning and rehearsals were over. Lt. Col. Fordham would say later "I knew the rescue operation would be a difficult one but I had total faith in the way it would be executed."

It was 0640hrs on Sunday September 10, 2000. In the pre-dawn darkness Mohammed Kamara, like all the West Side Boys, was unaware of the presence of the men of SGA in the jungle. Moments before gunfire erupted around the huts, above the sound of nocturnal insect life he detected in the distance the distinctive thudding beat of rotor blades as the Chinooks approached low over Rokel Creek. For the rescuers, now in flight, there had been an agonizing few minutes when SGA reported that they were still struggling through the dense jungle and had not reached a position

A WMIK, similar to those operated by the Royal Irish, manned by soldiers of 2 Royal Anglian passes a checkpoint manned by the SLA. A liaison officer from the SLA was captured along with The Royal Irish patrol and badly beaten by the West Side Boys. (IWM UKLC-2000-049-007-009)

where they could get a clear shot at the guards outside the White House, the camp commandant's house, where the Royal Irish were held. When they were in position the morning mist from Rokel Creek had not cleared and so the agonising delay lasted for a few more minutes. The helicopters went into a holding pattern over the Rokel Creek estuary and for a brief moment Capt. Danny Matthews wondered if the operation had been cancelled. Then the pilots received the signal that the SAS team was in position.

Thundering up the line of the river the helicopters were so low as they swung off towards their designated LZs that the down blast from the rotors ripped off the rusting corrugated iron roofs of the huts bordering the river and sent the tattered sheets careening across the jungle scrub. The roof on the White House collapsed under the down draft and trapped some West Side Boys beneath the twisted and rusty corrugated iron.

Kamara, who two days later walked in to a UN base to surrender, decided that discretion was the better part of valor and took cover in the jungle as the Lynx gunship swept in. "The helicopters were almost on the water," he said, "They fired again and again until there was no more shooting." By the time he emerged more than four hours later, many of his comrades were dead in the smoking wreckage that had been Gberi Bana and Magbeni.

Timing is essential in any military operation, and in Barras it meant the difference between success and catastrophe as, during the negotiations with Lt. Col. Fordham, Kallay had repeatedly threatened to kill the hostages if he heard helicopters approaching his jungle bases.

As the Chinook carrying the SAS hostage snatch team swept in and hovered above the palms in the half-light of dawn the West Side Boys at Gberi Bana opened fire. Corporal Blood described the attack:

> We never experienced anything like this … We saw the soldiers coming down to the ground. I fired my RPG two times, but both times the helicopter balanced [swerved] and I missed.

It may have been bad shooting by Corporal Blood or superb flying by the Chinook pilot such as he would demonstrate a few moments later. However, the team were now down safely and the helicopter had swung away out of range. Had Blood hit the helicopter with an RPG7 rocket, it would have been fatal and this casualty would have seriously jeopardized the operation.

SAS observation teams—discouraging interference

Moments before the West Side Boys started firing at the helicopter the SAS observation team SGA, now only 180 feet (55 m) from Gberi Bana, had opened fire on the men near the White House preventing them from killing the hostages. Progressing from observation and intelligence gathering they were now to "discourage any interference" until the main body arrived.

As the Chinooks started their final approach the pilots fired a barrage of infra-red (IR) flares. While these systems are designed to "spoof" Surface-to-Air Missiles like the SA7 "Guideline" shoulder-fired missile by producing a very hot signature that the missile's IR seeker will home on, during *Barras* they had another function. Although there was a possibility that SA7 might have reached the West Side Boys the main purpose of the flares was to confuse and frighten the men on the ground below. Fire from the Miniguns operated by the loadmasters aboard the Chinooks would

THE ASSAULT ON GBERI BANA AND MAGBENI

SEPTEMBER 10, 2000

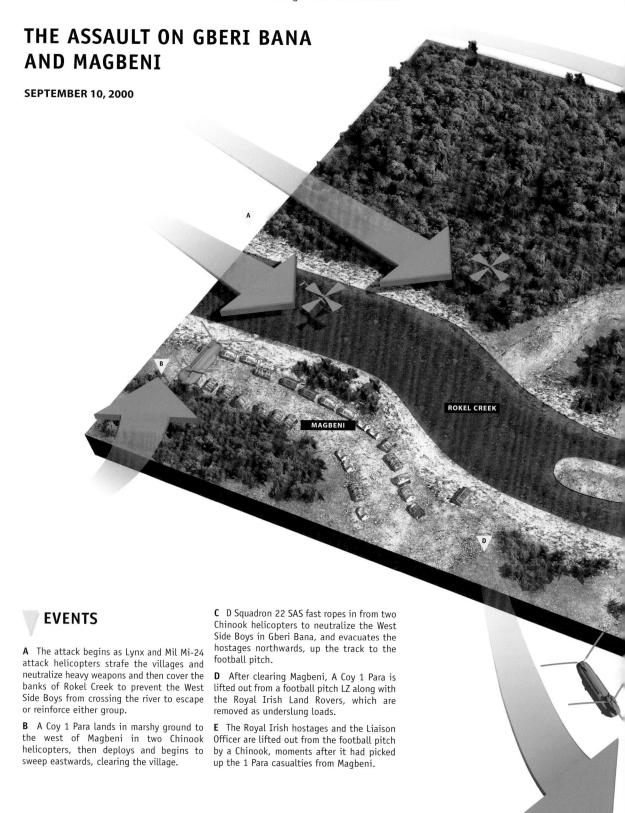

ROKEL CREEK

MAGBENI

▼ EVENTS

A The attack begins as Lynx and Mil Mi-24 attack helicopters strafe the villages and neutralize heavy weapons and then cover the banks of Rokel Creek to prevent the West Side Boys from crossing the river to escape or reinforce either group.

B A Coy 1 Para lands in marshy ground to the west of Magbeni in two Chinook helicopters, then deploys and begins to sweep eastwards, clearing the village.

C D Squadron 22 SAS fast ropes in from two Chinook helicopters to neutralize the West Side Boys in Gberi Bana, and evacuates the hostages northwards, up the track to the football pitch.

D After clearing Magbeni, A Coy 1 Para is lifted out from a football pitch LZ along with the Royal Irish Land Rovers, which are removed as underslung loads.

E The Royal Irish hostages and the Liaison Officer are lifted out from the football pitch by a Chinook, moments after it had picked up the 1 Para casualties from Magbeni.

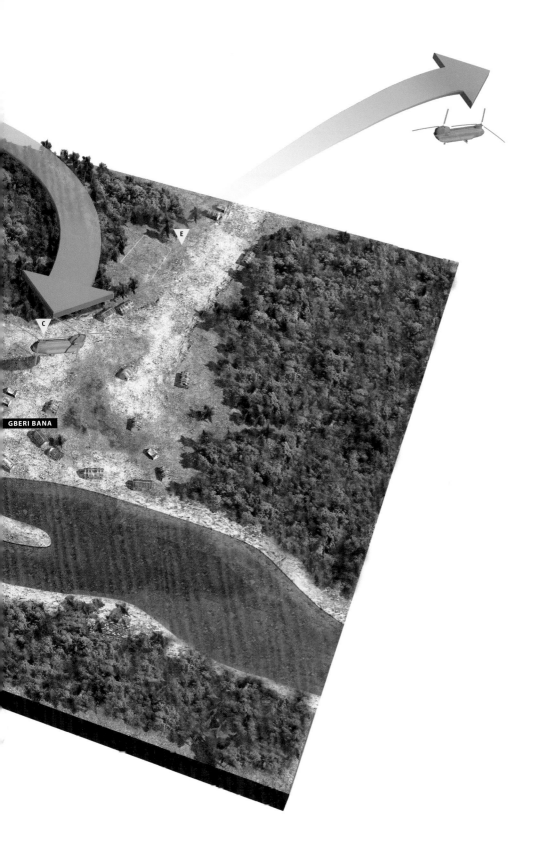

E

C

GBERI BANA

have added to the noise and violence of the insertion. It is little wonder then that when Kamara saw shapes descending rapidly from a helicopter he thought they were bombs. Only on a second glance did he realize they were the SAS teams fast roping into their LZs. It was probably in this initial ferocious firefight that Trooper Bradley "Brad" Tinnion was fatally wounded, hit by a .3-inch (7.62 mm) round that passed through his body and exited through his shoulder. Under heavy fire, his comrades dragged him to the Chinook and treated him as well as they could before he was evacuated. "Every effort was made to keep him alive," writes Tim Collins. "A needle was inserted through his ribs and connected to a two-pint drain to control the flow of blood into his chest and sustain his breathing." He died shortly after reaching operating theater aboard RFA *Sir Percivale*. It was when Tinnion's rank of Lance Bombardier and parent regiment, 29 Commando Regiment Royal Artillery, became public that it became evident to informed observers that *Barras* was a joint operation between the Parachute Regiment and the SAS. Tragically, *Barras* was Brad Tinnion's first operational mission with the SAS.

In the firefight that followed as the men of D Squadron cleared the buildings and surrounding jungle only two people escaped alive from Kallay's hut where he was subsequently found hiding under bedding and bodies.

"We didn't even realize we'd got Kallay. Those who fought, we killed. Those who surrendered, we captured. It was only later that we identified him," said a British officer after the raid. At the time it would probably have been easy for the two men from D Squadron who discovered Kallay to have killed him, but he did not resist and his capture would later prove to be a profound psychological victory.

It was reported that among those who died was "Mamy Kallay." Made of sterner stuff than her husband it was said that she was killed in action with a weapon in her hands. The news of her death was later greeted with delight by the former Sierra Leonean captives. However rumors later circulated in Freetown that she had survived, but had lost her mind and now, like an African Lady Macbeth, insane and incontinent, could be seen wandering the streets of the capital dressed in a soiled and tattered floral dress. Perhaps this was a more suitable end for someone whom a West Side Boys prisoner described as "A wicked, wicked woman."

Lying prone in the doorway of his hut Emmanuel Fabba, a prisoner of the West Side Boys, saw SAS fire teams blast buildings with 1.57-inch (40 mm) grenades fired from the M203 launchers on their Diemaco C7A1 rifles. One SAS trooper recalling the violent firefight said, "It was a bit like 'Gunfight at the OK Corral.'" Almost drowned out by the noise of the shooting and the overwhelming roar of the Chinooks the men of S10 could hear the shouts of "British Army! British Army!" from the Royal Irish.

The rescuers had a further task to locate Musa Bangura. The SAS trooper who found the SLA corporal in his squalid prison had to carry the young Sierra Leonean soldier who was weakened by beatings and starvation. Within 20 minutes the hostages had been released, raced through the firefight in Gberi Bana and were aboard the Chinook.

In Freetown officers at the JTFHQ could hear the gunfire over the radio loudspeakers as contact and casualty reports came in. It was now 0700hrs.

Enter 1 Para

As the Royal Irish were being rescued, across the muddy waters of Rokel Creek, at LZ2 at Magbeni the first Chinook lift inserted two platoons and HQ A Coy 1 Para who had packed into the helicopter. Though they knew the LZ would be marshy it was still a surprise when the first two soldiers jumped down from the rear ramp of a helicopter and plunged into a chest-deep swamp. The reeds had looked like grassland in aerial photographs and, though the map showed areas of permanent or seasonal marshland to the south and west, the terrain around LZ2 looked viable. The SAS patrol had seen water glinting through the grass but because of lack of cover and almost impenetrable secondary growth they were unable to get close enough to the LZ to establish the depth of the water.

Now what should have been a sprint to the tree line became a 328 foot to 492 foot (100 to 150 m) slog through mud and grass, with weapons held high, towards higher ground and the fringe of palms and scrub bordering the western end of the village that could be seen faintly in silhouette. "It was a massive pain..., but it wasn't unforeseen," remarked an officer after the action.

This was a moment when leadership came from the section commanders. With fire coming from the village the young corporals shouted encouragement to their sections and urged them to spread out and push through the swamp towards the trees.

> That was where the young NCOs were fantastic and that is where they really started gripping people. With the best will in the world the Company Commander and Platoon Commanders couldn't control it. They just wanted to focus on getting into the right point in the jungle.

As the Paras pushed forward they could feel the ground becoming firmer under foot and the swamp shallower. They hooked round to the left until they reached the tree line and were in position for the break into the village. They were wet and muddy and grass and reeds had clogged the linked GPMG ammunition that had been draped around the machine gunners. For CSM Chiswell, tasked with securing the LZ, there were several lonely minutes as his party waited in the swamp on the side closest to Magbeni for the next Chinook lift to come in five minutes later. It had flown back to Hastings to pick up the last elements of A Company Group and insert them at LZ2 before the CSM could move off to join the company.

A GPMG stolen from the SLA in the hands of a gang of West Side Boys. Though the West Side Boys had combated the RUF they had become a criminal gang terrorizing the country east of Freetown. (Corbis)

Twenty-two-year-old Capt. Matthews, the Company 2 IC, who came in on the second lift, admitted afterwards that like all the "Toms" he was apprehensive. "We knew the West Side Boys had lots of equipment, mortars, rifles, machine guns and heavy machine guns," he said, "There is obviously no set format and obviously that plays on your mind—not being able to predict your enemy's intentions or reactions." As the helicopter flared in he could see tracer fire: "We started taking incoming tracer fire from the ground and it was then that I realized that the people on the ground were actually going to fight."

The Army Air Corps Mk 7 Lynx AH helicopters blasted the West Side Boys' positions. Using the SS600 Series 3 Thermal Imager the crews picked up the cluster of men around the HMG firing at the 1 Para Chinook and raked it with machine gun fire until it was silent. The helicopters then moved in to cover the river. In addition to the British helicopters a Mil Mi-24 "Hind D" attack helicopter flown by Neall Ellis, a South African contract pilot, raked the village with rocket and cannon fire. For the men on the ground the streams of red tracer fire streaking down from the shadowy shape of the helicopters was reassuring as they shook out to assault the village.

Interviewed afterwards, one of the Para section commanders, 29 year-old Cpl. Simon Dawes, said simply, "We came under fire at first and then it was taken out. We had helicopters and we had heavy guns that suppressed the fire." Cpl. David Aitchinson, the young Scottish Para who was the company commander's radio operator, recalled that for a fraction of a second he paused on the ramp and looked at the sky laced with tracer fire and rockets as the SLA Hind D gunship and AAC Lynx helicopters raked the West Side Boys' village. It seemed to him a bit like a live firing exercise but one with an unimaginably greater intensity.

The company shook out to begin to clear through Magbeni sweeping from west to east. 3 Platoon successfully took Zulu, the first objective, a crumbling one-storey building. However, the fetid warmth of the jungle air was soon permeated with the sharp tang of burned cordite as resistance stiffened. The thump of exploding grenades and 2.6-inch (66 mm) LAWs punctuated the fast beat of GPMG fire and the sharper rattle of SA80 rifles firing on automatic. 2 Platoon came under heavy fire as it approached Yankee, the second objective.

First firefight

For many of the young Paras, this was their first experience of a sustained firefight. Cpl. Dawes said later, "This is the first firefight I have been in where rounds were coming my way." Interviewed in Freetown with the memory of the fighting still fresh he searched for words to describe the action and added modestly, "I don't like to talk about that sort of situation but it was scary. But once we got into the fighting the training took over."

When the company had returned to the UK, talking to Andy Simms of the British Army magazine *Soldier* Capt. Cradden was equally frank:

> Nothing prepares you for the operation we conducted ... I can safely say that I have never been as frightened. I was very frightened the night before, during deployment, and again when you see the casualties and injuries. It makes you realize that you can be hurt just like anyone else. Over that, the general perspective is that we each have a job to do and you cannot let your own personal emotions and private fears interfere with the fact that you are responsible for certain tasks.

Though the strafing runs by the attack helicopters had killed or frightened off some of the West Side Boys in Magbeni, a hard core were standing their ground and fighting back with determination. As the Company HQ Group moved forward to liaise with 2 Platoon there was an explosion.

"There was a loud explosion and we could hear these agonizing screams," said Pte. Sheard. Seven men had been injured but some might have been killed had they not been wearing helmets and body armor. The wounded included Maj. Lowe, who went down with shrapnel wounds to his legs, the 2 Platoon commander, and three of his HQ including Aitchinson, the OC's signaller. To Danny Matthews it looked as if the HQ group had dived for cover and his first thought was relief that they had survived and "You lucky bastards."

Of the explosion Damien Lewis writes in *Operation Certain Death*, "Although the Paras deny this, credible reports have it that the Paras actually mortared themselves, rather than being hit by an enemy mortar round." According to his source, an 'Operation *Barras* soldier' a mortar round on the upward trajectory hit the forest canopy. Lewis adds later, "Officially, however, the Paras maintain their command unit was hit by an enemy mortar round, and that is the most likely and credible version of events."

A less well-trained and led company might have been stalled by the loss of key commanders and communications links. What would now see the company through were the clear and concise orders that had been issued by Maj. Lowe.

"The OC called me up and told me I was to take over command of the company," Capt. Danny Matthews recalled. Capt. Matthews could see that the blast had stripped the combat trousers off the company commander. It was like a preplanned phase of a field training exercise in which the Directing Staff remove key players in the command structure and pitch subordinate officers and NCOs into these positions. However, this time it was for real.

Captain Matthews takes command

Capt. Matthews thought fast; weapons and ammunition were removed from the wounded and the radios from the signalers and they were dragged to cover:

> I cracked on to find the platoon sergeant pushing one of his sections through the attack at the timer and he called back to me. "Where's the boss?" I told him he was the boss. He said, "Where's the OC?," and I said, "I'm the OC, let's push on."

As a radio operator transmitted the Casualty Report the crew of the Chinook, inbound to pick up the hostages, heard the message. An orange smoke grenade was "popped" and, in a piece of superb flying, the helicopter landed on the track in the village under fire. The wounded were quickly loaded on board and were on their way to Freetown and *Sir Percivale*. For the Paras on the ground the helicopter casualty evacuation was dramatic and also hazardous as the down wash from the rotors pealed the roof off a building close to where they had taken up positions, sending sheets of corrugated iron and timber crashing down.

Casualty evacuation

The casualty evacuation was so fast that Capt. Thomas the RMO and the Company Aid Post were still running towards the site of the explosion when the helicopter lifted off. After the initial cries of pain the wounded Paras were now grimly silent. Some had been able to walk onto the helicopter but others had had to be supported aboard. Here men of the Field Surgical Team from 16 Close Support Medical Regiment RAMC worked hard to stabilize injuries. The speed of the evacuation

OVERLEAF
The fight for Magbeni. While some of the huts in the village were habitable, many had collapsed and were in ruins—all of them, however, offered cover to the West Side Boys. The men of A Company 1 Para used the buildings and the elephant grass bordering the village for cover, and worked forward in bounds giving one another cover as they moved. While the West Side Boys may not have employed conventional tactics, they were determined fighters who were not afraid to die. The Paras made a phased attack through the village, moving from west to east, clearing buildings and driving the West Side Boys out of Magbeni to secure the south bank of Rokel Creek and then destroy the weapons and ammunition stocks held by the gang.

ensured that the wounded reached the operating theater on board *Sir Percivale* within 20 minutes of being injured.

When the A Coy plans were being prepared it had been decided that radio communications would be in clear—though the West Side Boys might have had the captured radio from the Royal Irish patrol, if by chance they were on the same frequency they would not have time to react to any signals they intercepted. The speed and simplicity of this net probably contributed to the quick reactions of the Chinook crew.

The first casualties arrived at 0630hrs and a total of 13 were received on the RFA. While some were treated for minor injuries, the medical team also performed emergency surgery. All patients had been treated and stabilized by 1830hrs and were ready to be flown to the Royal Naval Hospital Haslar in Portsmouth, England. Surgeon Lt. Carty said, "Although we train for this kind of thing, I would be lying if I didn't say that it was very stressful at times."

Inside the Chinook, 1 Para casualties had the satisfaction of knowing that *Barras* was a success. It swung across the river to land at the football pitch by the ferry point and Cpl. Aitchinson remembered the hostages boarding the helicopter with the SAS team covering the pickup. He summed up everyone's feelings succinctly: "It was a case of a good job done." From here they were flown to *Sir Percivale* for medical checks and the start of the debriefing on their mission.

The loss of key members of the A Coy HQ might have stalled the attack and caused it to lose momentum against increasingly aggressive West Side Boys opposition. Interviewed some years later Matthews commented, "Having seized the initiative and gained the momentum what you can't afford is to lose momentum and slow down." However, A Coy kept up the momentum with 2 Platoon securing objective Yankee as 3 Platoon moved parallel with them. Initially, the GPMG gunners had problems with stoppages because their link had fouled with grass and mud, but they worked quickly to clear the weapons. They then engaged the West Side Boys' positions, firing the 25.7-pound (11.65 kg) machine gun from the shoulder because the thick vegetation made it impossible to see targets while firing from the prone position.

They had realized that this would be necessary during rehearsals at Hastings and had practiced hard during the work up for the operation. Under cover of smoke from Red Phosphorus grenades, 1 Platoon dashed across the open track. By now the West Side Boys could be seen withdrawing eastwards towards LZ1 and the lead platoon concentrated its fire on the fleeting targets.

1 Platoon assaulted X-Ray and Whiskey close to Rokel Creek. At Whiskey they found the West Side Boys' ammunition dump, professionally dug in with a poncho stretched above it. 3 Platoon then cleared Victor, Uniform and Tango, the buildings south of the track and moved into a blocking position to cover any counterattacks from the West Side Boys' units around Laia Junction. The immersion in the swampy LZ at the outset of the operation had caused some problems

A sight that would terrify travelers on the roads outside the capital. Groups like this would stop and rob civilians and exercise a rule of fear in the area. From people who were already poor they would steal what little they owned. (Corbis)

with the radios, but if electronic communications were unreliable, the human voice worked effectively in the small area of the village. The action had been a classic corporal's war fought by small well-led groups of soldiers.

Clearance patrols were mounted by 1 Platoon. They pushed out into the secondary jungle to find any West Side Boys who might have concealed themselves, but after 66 feet (20 m) the vegetation became too dense.

Magbeni secured

It was now 0800hrs and Magbeni was secure. The company took up defensive positions, set up Claymore mines to cover their arcs and paid out the brown cable from the mines back to their shell scrapes.

The Mortar Section was now flown in to LZ2, but since there was no suitable position for the base plates it was flown to LZ1. Here they found difficulty adjusting their fire because the dense vegetation concealed the "splash" of dirt and smoke from the exploding HE mortar bombs and the fall of shot could not be seen even when smoke rounds were fired. The Mortar Fire Controller was picked up by a Lynx but unfortunately now there were difficulties with signals. The solution was to correct fire by the rather hazardous expedient of aural adjustment. This involves listening for the direction and loudness of the impact and adjusting the elevation and alignment of the barrel. With minimum charge and barrels elevated almost to the vertical the bombs fell on the Final Protective Fire target close to the forward positions. If there were going to be a West Side Boy counterattack it was here that the interlocking fire from the GPMGs, the blast of the Claymores and aimed rifle fire would halt them. The mortars could bring down fire not only around Magbeni but also across the river at Gberi Bana.

A patrol now moved through the village destroying vehicles including the Bedford with the ZPU-2, which required a substantial charge to wreck it effectively. In the end it took three "Technicals" and ammunition including large stocks of mortar ammunition and RPG rounds with PE4 Plastic Explosives. Petrol or RP grenades were used to burn down buildings. The West Side Boys' armory was a mixture of Soviet and British weapons; the former had filtered through Liberia from Libya. The British weapons, notably the L1A1 Self Loading Rifle (SLR) and the L7A2 GPMG, had come from stocks stolen from the SLA.[5]

A Company Group had completed its mission and as the main body went firm around LZ1, Capt. Matthews with two sections led a final sweep through the village.

Across the river 15 male and three female prisoners were taken. Their wrists secured with white plasticuffs they were bundled, along with the bodies of their dead comrades, into the Chinooks. The prisoners were then passed to the UNAMSIL Jordanian Battalion and thence to the Sierra Leonean Police.

Twenty-five West Side Boys died during the raid. Officially, three of the dead were women but the real figure seems more likely to have been five. One source close to the operation said the death toll was probably higher. The resistance put up by the West Side Boys had actually been much stronger than had been expected. Cornered, some of the gang had fought with little thought of surrender. "If you followed every blood trail into the jungle you might well be able to quadruple that figure."

---

5 In his autobiography *Rules of Engagement A Life in Conflict* Tim Collins noted that 1 Para decided that two SLRs used by the West Side Boys could be deactivated and retained by the battalion as trophies. It was only when they had returned to the UK that they discovered that the serial number on one rifle corresponded with one originally held in their armory in 1972. It was in that year that 13 Civil Rights protesters had been shot dead in Londonderry in Northern Ireland on January 30 by men of 1 Para in what became known as "Bloody Sunday." Controversially it had been reported to the Saville Inquiry into the events of "Bloody Sunday" that was sitting in 2000 that all the weapons held by 1 Para in 1972 had been destroyed.

The prisoners were taken by D Squadron on the north bank because the conditions that had made Gberi Bana an ideal prison—the creek to the south and jungle and swamp to east and west—now gave them nowhere to run as the SAS swept through the village.

Across the river A Coy had fulfilled its mission of defeating the West Side Boys within their area of responsibility and there was no call to pursue and destroy the gang. When the attack started before dawn at Magbeni and the darkness had filled with tracer and the thump of explosions from the rockets, the assault on the senses would have been overwhelming. Realizing that they were up against not nervous or compliant UNAMSIL troops but the overwhelming, controlled violence of professional soldiers, many of the West Side Boys had fled in the darkness and the first light of the misty dawn to hiding places in the jungle.

Sierra Leonean hostages released

What went largely unreported by the British media was that the raid also freed 22 Sierra Leoneans held prisoner for weeks or even months. Five were women abducted and forced to become cooks, "bush wives" or "sex combatants"—West Side Boys terms for women coerced into sexual relationships. The men had been used as forced labor or put through a crude form of military training.

The female Sierra Leonean captives were kept across the river at Magbeni. If Operation *Barras* had not been launched, the "sex combatants" and the male prisoners would probably have been murdered when they were no longer useful, or have died of disease. If the negotiations had succeeded and the British soldiers had walked free, or been released by a covert Special Forces operation, the Africans would certainly have died. The rescue of the British on these terms might have been a tactical success but would have risked becoming a strategic surrender to the forces of anarchy.

The Royal Irish soldiers had initially been held in a building identified as Colonel Cambodia's house but were moved on Friday September 1 to the camp commandant's house. Here they spent much of their time under guard in a 42.6 feet (13 m) x 7.8 feet (2.4 m) room in a cement-and-mud house, the home of the former village chief. The building, dubbed "The White House" by the British planners, must have been quite stylish with a pillared veranda and steep pitched roof. Now it was battered and dilapidated with a rusty corrugated iron roof and no longer weatherproof. Inside there were mats and blankets for the soldiers' bedding. Armed guards kept watch by the door and window and the SAS observation team had identified a Soviet-era .5-inch (12.72 mm) DshK HMG covering the building. The only lavatory was a hole in the ground in a metal hut that was shared by captives and militiamen. Emmanuel Fabba, a West Side Boys prisoner, said that in the week he was there the soldiers were taken to wash once in the nearby Rokel Creek. He said:

> They washed themselves and their uniforms, which they put back on wet. Usually, the British kept very quiet. They spoke to each other in low voices and sometimes shared a cigarette. The Major did the talking for them if he needed to speak with the West Side Boys.

For meals the British soldiers mixed tinned British Army Composition or "compo" rations sent in by the negotiation team with local bush food such as cassava leaves and coconuts. The militiamen also treated their captives to sachets of cheap gin, known by the fighters as "morale-boosters."

According to Fabba, the British soldiers were pushed and threatened but not assaulted. In contrast, Bangura the Sierra Leonean LO had been badly beaten and held in an open pit covered with a wooden grid. Men and women from the West Side Boys had then relieved themselves into the pit. To the drug- and drink-clouded minds of the men and women of the West Side Boys the unfortunate Bangura was a "traitor."

Fabba reported that, prior to Operation *Barras*, Maj. Marshall assured him and his fellow captives that there would be a rescue mission. After the operation had been successfully concluded, the media reported that Lt. Col. Fordham had warned Marshall about the planned hostage rescue operation possibly by veiled speech in an innocent expression of affection: "Sally and Sarah send their regards and so does Dawn." The SAS were coming at first light.

In reality, to ensure security no warning was given to the hostages and even the negotiating team were not told about the operation. In the planning stage there had been some discussion about using the SLA to form an outer cordon around the villages. Their mission would be code named Operation *Amble*. This would give the SLA some credit for playing a part in the operation—while this would have been sound politics and would have enhanced the standing of the government in Freetown and the SLA, it was dropped at the request of the CDS Gen. Sir Charles Guthrie, arguably because of the risk of compromising operational security and to keep the complex operation as simple as possible.

It is, however, possible that with their rank and experience the soldiers of the Royal Irish surmised that the time was approaching when direct action would be necessary and Marshall sensibly decided to let the Sierra Leonean hostages know what to do when the assault happened. Fabba explained:

> He came to talk to me in a low voice. He pointed at the wings on his uniform and said the Paras were coming. He did not know exactly when, but he said we should not leave the house when we heard the helicopters. We knew the British were our only hope and had prayed that they would come soon as the West Side Boys had threatened to execute us.

At dawn on Sunday, the Sierra Leonean hostages survived by lying pressed to the floors inside their huts when the silence was filled with gunfire and the thump of the rotors of the hovering Chinook as the SAS teams attacked. Overcome by this terrifying assault on his senses one captive, Braima Phohba, a student at Bunumbu Teachers' College, panicked, ran from the hut and was caught in the cross-fire and killed.

Fabba went on to describe that morning:

> There was so much shouting and shooting, it was terrible. We saw a British soldier outside, so we called out, "Civilian hostages, don't shoot." They brought us out of the back of the building, tied us up and made us lie face down in case we were West Side Boys. The Major confirmed our identity later.

For the British hostages it was essential that they identify themselves to their rescuers in the noise and violence. Their shouts of "British soldiers! British soldiers!" were greeted by a reassuring shout of "British Army" by the men of D Squadron. The rescuers then asked where the SLA Corporal was located and the battered, soiled, but alive Cpl. Musa Bangura was dragged from his squalid prison.

For Binta Sesay, Contobie's nine-months pregnant wife, the timing of the attack saved her life and that of her unborn child. Her husband had said he was going to kill her on Monday because she had urged him to surrender. Binta had struggled under a bed when the SAS attack hit Gberi Bana. "I was very afraid, but the soldier spoke to me quietly. He brought me water, lit a cigarette and asked me if I wanted one. He was a friendly man."

With the two areas secured the Chinooks began to shuttle West Side Boys prisoners and dead out of the area.

Across the creek the Paras had located the three Royal Irish Land Rovers and found that, despite some bullet holes in the bodywork and flat tyres, they could still be driven. A helicopter returned from BTC with spare keys for the vehicles. They were then driven to LZ1, rigged for underslinging and lifted out by a Chinook. The Browning HMG on the WMIK had not been fired because the young Ranger who had been manning it when the patrol was ambushed had quickly disabled the gun.

It was now 1100hrs.

1 Para liftoff

As the heat increased, the last helicopters carrying the men of D Squadron and 1 Para lifted off in a swirl of dust and leaves and twisting columns of smoke. Now the survivors of the West Side Boys crawled from the jungle around Gberi Bana and surveyed the destruction and carnage.

"There were many corpses and wounded people lying on the ground moaning," said 16-year-old Unisa Sesay, a member of the gang's Small Boys Unit. "One commander was standing and his friend was trying to remove a fragment from his shoulder. The rest of the people were on the ground."

Cyrus, a 17-year-old boy soldier, claimed they had been told the wounded would be shot and thrown into the river because there were no medical supplies. Both boys said they had seen too many corpses and were too shocked to count. They reported that the dead included a Sierra Leonean hostage and a boy of about 14 from the SBU.

Subsequently, an estimated 50 child soldiers who had fled the fighting went into hiding in the surrounding bush. Fearful travellers along the road from Freetown's peninsula to the interior claimed to have spotted armed boys as young as eight roaming through the jungle.

Alieu Sissay, who had encountered them on the road, said, "We wanted to try to coax them out and one or two of us shouted to them, but they just vanished. No one is going to go in there to get them the help they need."

He described how the smallest in the group, carrying an AK47 and dressed in underpants and a torn T-shirt, had poked his face out from behind a large leaf and smiled. Another child pulled him back into the thicket. "They have no conscience and they have done terrible things," said Sissay.

The Royal Fleet Auxiliary *Sir Percivale*, the invaluable "Percy," a ship that would play a critical role as a secure logistics base in Operation *Barras*. (Author's Collection)

In the security of Freetown the six released Royal Irish hostages had been reunited with their five comrades from the ill-fated patrol. They telephoned their families and went through a range of medical checks on board *Sir Percivale*.

Lt. Col. Fordham described the condition of the six:

> I saw them on the ship this morning and they looked remarkably well considering the ordeal they had been through. These are soldiers that fell back on training and it demonstrates how good these men were in terms of their strength of character and spirit of endeavor. They are physically and mentally exhausted and need time to recover. They were kept in very poor conditions and they looked after themselves as best they could. They were given little freedom of movement and their basic requirements of food and water were severely limited. When the first five came out they recounted an incident of a mock execution, but it was not repeated. I told representatives of the militia group that I would not tolerate any abuse of the soldiers.

For the men of A Coy now aboard the RFA *Argus*, "a post operational amount of alcohol was drunk in celebration." In fact to the surprise of the crew of *Argus*, after a few beers many of the tired Toms were pleased to be able to clean up and get to sleep. The following day they boarded C-130s at Freetown before changing to an RAF Tristar at Dakar for the final leg back to the UK, arriving back early on the morning of Tuesday September 11.

DSF and his HQ along with D Squadron also made their exit on Monday morning. Within less than 24 hours the word was out in Freetown that the West Side Boys had been defeated. Now the crews of British military vehicles driving through Freetown and the outlying villages were greeted with broad smiles, waves and applause.

Foday Kallay, in the custody of the Sierra Leonean Police, recorded a radio message calling on his followers to give up the fight and go to UN demobilization camps before they were hunted down. The two policemen who took down Kallay's statement used an unorthodox approach to encourage him to cooperate. One threatened to cut off his arms just as his followers had hacked off the limbs of innocent Sierra Leoneans. The other proposed a more humane course—if Kallay did not assist the investigation the police would simply dump him on a street corner and the citizens of Freetown could exercise justice.

In the afternoon following *Barras*, 30 West Side Boys had already surrendered to the men of JordBat 2 at Masiaka. Two days later, 18 surrendered to Jordanian peacekeepers at Magbuntoso, 24.8 miles (40 km) east of Freetown. By September 22 a total of 371 demoralized West Side Boys, including 57 child soldiers, had been disarmed.

In the police headquarters in Freetown Kallay, dressed only in an oversized filthy fake Calvin Klein T-shirt that almost covered his grubby boxer shorts, stood impassively with his hands handcuffed behind his back and identified the bodies of his former comrades in arms. After identification they were loaded into a truck and driven to a mass grave. It was the end of the West Side Boys.

As the West Side Boys trailed in to surrender in the months following the operation, some volunteered for the new SLA. Following screening those who were accepted were posted to Benguema to begin their training. Here an instructor from the Light Infantry discovering that one of his students was a former West Side Boy couldn't resist asking about Operation *Barras*—though he chose a rather nuanced approach.

"How did you find the SAS?" he asked.

"The SAS found us," came the slightly puzzled reply.

CONCLUSION

By a remarkable coincidence, in London on Sunday morning September 10 the Chief of the Defence Staff had been booked to give a live interview for the high profile BBC 1 television current affairs program "Breakfast with Frost."

The interview with Gen. Guthrie had been arranged in June and at the time it was assumed it would address general issues about the role of the British Armed Forces.

On Sunday morning in the studio at the BBC Television Centre, Shepherds Bush, there was an increasing tension as the general was running late. The veteran broadcaster and journalist Sir David Frost, the program presenter, was playing for time by reviewing the Sunday papers when Guthrie arrived at the Television Centre. Switching off his secure mobile phone, through which he had been monitoring the operation, he emerged languidly from his staff car and, as the producer described to me some years later, apologized for his delay with elegant understatement:

I'm sorry I'm late there's been a bit of trouble in Africa.

At about 0920hrs in London, Maj. Tom Thornycroft had confirmed to Guthrie that all the hostages were safe. The television production team hurried to check if the story was being covered by any of the international news agencies—there was nothing on the wires. "There probably won't be anything out for about an hour," commented Guthrie.

For Frost the drama of the moment was compelling:

Now it's very rare that you get dramatic breaking military news and the key figure of the moment coinciding live while we're on the air, the two together is really rare but that's just what's happening here this morning. In the last few minutes we've learned that British soldiers in Sierra Leone have this morning undertaken military action aimed at releasing the British hostages who have been held in the jungle for the last fortnight. There's nothing on the wires yet, nothing is publicly known but the man who knows more than anyone else, who has the latest information is with us, he's the head of the Army and the Navy and the Air Force, General Sir Charles Guthrie, good morning Charles, this sounds like amazing breaking news, good news.

Guthrie was measured in his reply:

Well I hope it's good news, we think it's good news. We decided to attack the place where the hostages were being kept at half past six this morning.

He went on:

So the situation is still very confused, there is fighting going on but the first indications are that the hostages are safe, I don't know what condition they're in but they are safe. I don't know whether we've had any casualties, we didn't want to have to do this, we didn't want to have to assault because it's a very difficult operation, there are big risks in it but we have done it and the reason we did it is because really our negotiations were getting nowhere. The hostages had been there for three weeks, they were threatening to kill them, or they were threatening to move them to different parts of Sierra Leone and once they'd done that we'd never be able to recover from with ease, which I hope we've done this morning.

So it's very difficult, but I do want to stress this is a very, very tricky, complicated operation we're doing a long way away in very difficult terrain where, working as a team with the Foreign Office, with the police our ministers have had some tough decisions to take because if it goes wrong we're in trouble.

"This kind of operation is never without risk," he later explained at a press conference at the MoD. "We are not playing some stupid arcade game ... The West Side Boys were not a pushover. They fought very hard. We did not want to do this, but the clock started turning."

In fact, as Guthrie was talking to Frost Operation *Barras* still had about an hour to run as the SAS cleared Gberi Bana, assembled the prisoners and destroyed the captured weapons and equipment. As a senior officer closely involved in the operation commented afterwards:

> Until Guthrie spoke, no one in Freetown knew what was going on and the hacks were still in the hotel recovering from their Saturday night hangovers ... As it happened it didn't cause any problems and probably got Guthrie out of a few awkward questions from Frost on the Defence Budget!

There was a discreet delay before some of the decorations awarded to men who had participated in Operation *Barras* were made public. All the awards were gazetted with the date April 6, 2002.

In addition to the gallantry awards a number of other decorations and honors were given, ranging from appointments to the Order of the British Empire to Mentions in Despatches and the Queen's Commendation for Valuable Service.

There might have been a delay in publishing the decorations and awards but the MoD was quick to issue a press release on *Barras*, albeit one that made no reference to the crucial role of D Squadron 22 SAS. Like other reports this gave the impression to the general public that the rescue operation had been conducted entirely by 1 Para.

Distinguished Service Order	Major General John Taylor Holmes OBE MC Brigadier David Julian Richards CBE
Conspicuous Gallantry Cross	Color Sergeant John David Baycroft MBE, Parachute Regiment Squadron Leader Iain James McKechnie MacFarlane, Royal Air Force
Distinguished Service Cross	Captain George Michael Zambellas, Royal Navy
Military Cross	Warrant Officer Class II Harry William Bartlett, Parachute Regiment Major James Robert Chiswell, Parachute Regiment Captain Evan John Jeaffreson Fuery, Parachute Regiment Sergeant Stephen Michael Christopher Heaney, Parachute Regiment Acting Captain Daniel John Matthews, Parachute Regiment
Distinguished Flying Cross	Flight Lieutenant Timothy James Burgess, Royal Air Force Squadron Leader Iain James McKechnie MacFarlane, Royal Air Force Captain Allan Laughlan Moyes, Army Air Corps Flight Lieutenant Jonathan Priest, Royal Air Force Flight Lieutenant Paul Graham Shepherd, Royal Air Force
Queen's Gallantry Medal	Major Philip Conyers Ashby, Royal Marines, for services in May 2000

MINISTRY OF DEFENCE PRESS RELEASE – 1630HRS, SEPTEMBER 10, 2000

The objective of this release is to provide further details of the military operation that took place this morning to secure the release of the seven hostages being held by the West Side Boys in Sierra Leone.

Introduction

The Secretary of State made clear this afternoon that the decision to launch an operation to release the hostages was only undertaken when it became apparent that the threat to the hostages had escalated to the point that it overcame the risk of conducting the rescue operation. The Chief of the Defence Staff had indicated earlier in the day that there had been a number of British casualties. We regret to confirm that during the action the UK did sustain a number of casualties. One soldier has been killed, one soldier received serious injuries that are not thought to be life threatening and 11 other soldiers were injured. All casualties have been stabilized following treatment by British medical teams who were in support of the operation. Next of Kin have been informed. Hostages and casualties will be moved back to the UK as soon as possible.

Background

The risks associated with undertaking any hostage release operation are very real in any circumstances.
As was stated by the Chief of the Defence Staff this morning, the particular circumstances in Sierra Leone made this one of the most complex operations UK forces have conducted for many years. The West Side Boys are a very unpredictable, well armed and volatile group. They have a hard core of highly experienced jungle fighters. The terrain was also highly challenging. Gberi Bana the rebel camp is in a village on the north bank of the Rokel Creek. The camp is surrounded to the North and West by dense secondary jungle and overgrown palm plantations. To the East is a large area of swamp. Across the creek are the villages of Magbeni and Forodugu.

The Operation

The operation was initiated at 0616 hrs this morning, following detailed planning both in the UK and in theater. Members of all three Services were involved in the operation. The assault included elements of the 1st Battalion of the Parachute Regiment, Lynx Attack Helicopters and RAF Chinook helicopters, armed for self defence. Assistance was also provided by the Sierra Leone Army and the UN mission in Sierra Leone, particularly the Jordanian battalion, which provided security along the Maslaka highway. The assault itself involved a co-ordinated two prong helicopter assault against the rebel Headquarters in Gberi Bana and the West Side Boys units located in the villages of Magbeni and Forodugu. The northern phase of the assault aimed to release the hostages thought to be at Gberi Bana. The aim of the Southern phase was to neutralize the enemy position on the southern bank of the Rokel Creek that was equipped with HMGs that posed a significant threat to our aircraft.

Outcome of the Operation

The assault on Gberi Bana was highly successful. All seven hostages (including the Sierra Leonean Officer) were successfully and rapidly released unharmed and are now safely on board RFA *Sir Percivale*. All British hostages have spoken to their families by telephone. The Southern assault was also successful in preventing West Side Boy units South of Rokel Creek from interdicting the hostages as they were airlifted out. This involved the clearance of the rebel camps and involved suppressive fire as the advances took place. Our troops came under sustained fire including from the edge of the jungle. This in turn was countered by our own mortar fire. This action also led to the recovery of the UK vehicles held by the West Side Boys. All UK forces involved in the operation have now left the Gberi Bana region and will return to the UK as soon as possible.

Enemy forces

The West Side Boys fought fiercely throughout the operation and engaged in sporadic follow up fighting for some time whilst the UK forces were preparing for their self extraction having released the hostages.

Casualties

Details of West Side Boy casualties remain unclear, however, we can confirm over 25 dead including 3 females.

Conclusion

To conclude, this was a very challenging operation conducted out of necessity because of the serious threat to the lives of the hostages. Despite being an operation of great complexity, thousands of miles from the UK, all our mission objectives were achieved. This is a testimony to the skill and professionalism of all those involved. The Prime Minister, Mr Tony Blair, said "I cannot pay high enough tribute to the skill, the professionalism and the courage of the armed forces involved."

ANALYSIS

In postoperation analysis of Operation *Barras* by some of the Special Forces, it was reckoned that the full-blooded attack by the Paras had been unnecessary. In a variant of the deliberate plan, the guards could have been killed silently at night and the hostages extracted covertly and exfiltrated from the West Side Boys' camp down Rokel Creek by inflatable craft. This, however, does not take account of the sand banks and current in Rokel Creek, the unpredictable routine in Gberi Bana or the problems of making a stealthy approach through dense vegetation.

Unofficially, even the MoD acknowledged that they were relieved that *Barras* had suffered only one death and 12 injuries, 11 of them minor. One veteran SAS officer characterized the operation as "not a clinical, black balaclava, Princess Gate type operation. It was a very grubby, green operation with lots of potential for things to go wrong." However, as Connaughton commented, "One lesson these unfortunate casualties established was that the UK government was not casualty averse in circumstances where the cause was just."

Some of the British media, while celebrating the success of Operation *Barras*, were quick to blame Maj. Marshall. If he had not taken the patrol off the main road to investigate the situation of the West Side Boys the Royal Irish would not have been captured. The UNAMSIL HQ, which had an uneasy relationship with the British, placed the blame on Marshall with the CO of JordBat 2 denying that he had requested that the major visit the West Side Boys' camp.

With the Royal Irish now safe in Freetown, Brig Peter Pearson, a senior aide to Gen. Sir Mike Jackson, then Commander Land [formerly UK Land Command], flew out to debrief the men. His report described the events that led up to their capture and concluded that:

> Major Alan Marshall made an error of professional judgement in diverting from a planned and authorized journey so as to make an unauthorized visit to the village of Magbeni. There his patrol was overwhelmed. Maj Marshall made a grave mistake.

The mix of ex-soldiers and criminals who made up the West Side Boys is illustrated by this group, which includes a man sporting an SLA beret. All appear to have had weapon training by the way in which they are handling their ex-SLA SLRs. (Corbis)

In Freetown the press reported that senior British defense sources said that:

> [Major Allan Marshall] has repeated at the start and finish of every conversation that he absolutely accepts as the company commander full responsibility.

The men of A Coy justly received the plaudits of a grateful government, and D Squadron slipped quietly away as is the practice of UK Special Forces. However, as Tim Collins observes:

> Sadly for the men of 1 R Irish, while the media and the British military hierarchy celebrated the success of the rescue, they virtually ignored the men who had been held in captivity. The only people who showed any interest in them were Brigadier Peter Wall, Commander 16 Air Assault Brigade, and the Colonel-in-Chief, His Royal Highness the Duke of York. Not for the first time, the men and their families had reason to thank this frequent visitor. The battalion was delighted to receive warm messages of congratulations from the President of Ireland, Mary McAleese. From the British Government there wasn't a word.

Musa Bangura, who had been brutally beaten by the West Side Boys, received a week's sick leave. After seven days the courageous Sierra Leonean NCO, who would later be commissioned, reported back for duty at Benguema. However, it would be a month before he could stretch his arms out fully and for many months he feared his hands would be paralyzed.

At a press conference in the capital the 28-year-old Bangura was passionate in his defense of Maj. Marshall and the Royal Irish patrol. Bangura insisted that the colonel at JordBat 2 had asked the British to take "a closer look" at the area and that the two officers on the patrol had been given "assurances" before they drove off the highway into the Okra Hill area.

Quoted in *Operation Certain Death* Bangura said of Marshall:

> He should have had many years of brilliant work ahead of him, as a professional soldier. Now it looks as though his career is over. There were times when we were certain we would be killed, but he did not let us despair. He was kind and courageous and never complained about his own suffering. I thank Alan Marshall for saving my life. I would like to think that one day I could be as good a soldier as he is.

A few years later Marshall received praise for his conduct from an officer well placed to comment on the operation. He told me that:

> Marshall could not have predicted that the West Side Boys would react in the way that they did. The same could have happened to numerous other similar patrols elsewhere in Sierra Leone. On a different day they would probably have reacted differently, and nothing would have been heard of it.

> Perhaps his patrol could have deployed differently when they went into the village, with a team covering from way back as he went forward, and therefore they all wouldn't have been so quickly swamped. But even then it would have been difficult for the cover team to extract those who had been taken. Casualties would probably have been high, including members of the patrol.

> It is easy for officers safe back in LAND Command and MoD to second guess what

Marshall should or should not have done, and to talk of him making a "grave mistake" in exercising his initiative. They were not the men on the ground—he was. Even if the route and visit had been planned and registered it would not have prevented his capture. Indeed, any number of other patrols could conceivably have ended up in a similar set of circumstances. All these operations rely on the use of initiative.

> We rely on men such as these [Marshall] to stick their necks out in operations across the world

He added:

> We must therefore be prepared sometimes for things not always to go according to plan. That is why we have contingencies, and they must have the confidence that we will back them up—come what may. The British Army punches above its weight in many areas. If we lose the courage and "brass neck" of our soldiers we will all join the ranks of mediocrity—and there are plenty of armies already in that vein.

The success of A Coy 1 Para during Operation *Barras* was one of the drivers for the establishment of the Special Forces Support Group (SFSG), which was formed officially on April 3, 2006.

Based at RAF St. Athan near Cardiff in Wales, the force has a strength of between 450 and 1, 200. Though personnel continue to wear their own cap badge, SFSG has a distinctive flash showing a silver dagger on a green background with a red lined black flash of lightning running through it.

The SFSG is a force multiplier for Special Forces. Its roles are acting as a quick reaction force for SAS/SBS operations, sealing off and guarding an area of operation, taking part in large scale assaults alongside SAS/SBS forces, carrying out secondary assaults and diversionary raids, acting as a "blocking force" against counter attacks, CBRN detection/protection, and domestic antiterrorist support.

All, bar the Chemical Biological Radiological and Nuclear (CBRN) team who are drawn from the RAF Regiment, are parachute trained. Perhaps appropriately after the success of Operation *Barras* the SFSG is built around 1 Para and the orbat is as follows:

Headquarters (HQ) Company
Four Strike Companies
A Coy (1 Para)
B Coy (1 Para + a platoon of RAF Regiment)
C Coy (1 Para)
F Coy (Royal Marines)
Support Company
attached / supporting units
RAF Regiment Forward Air Controllers
RAF Regiment CBRN unit
268 (SFSG) Signals Squadron
elements of 539 ASRM

Since its formation it has been reported that SFSG has been employed on operations in Iraq and Afghanistan. In the course of time line infantry regiments will replace 1 Para in the SFSG role.

GLOSSARY

alphanumeric Passwords consisting of letters (alpha) and numbers (numeric).

battalion A large military group or unit.

brigadier A British officer who commands a brigade.

Chinook A type of military helicopter that has two propellers and is capable of heavy lifts.

coup An overthrow of a government or ruling group.

democracy A form of government that is run by the voting power of the majority.

insurgent A person who acts against, in a political way, a civil authority or a political group.

operation A mission, usually military in nature.

Operation *Barras* The rescue mission initiated by the British military in Sierra Leone on September 10, 2000.

rebel Someone who acts in opposition to authority.

reconnaissance A military strategy to infiltrate enemy territory to gain intelligence, or information.

refugee A person taking refuge, or fleeing the danger of a country or power.

regime A form of government or a government that is currently in power.

republic A form of government usually consisting of a president as it's head of state and system in which the majority has voting power.

Royal Marines Also known as Corps of Her Majesty's Royal Marines, the amphibious branch of the military of the United Kingdom.

SAS (Special Air Service) The special forces branch of the British military.

Sierra Leone A former British colony and now a republic in West Africa with a population of approximately 5.2 million people.

terror The act of instilling fear into a group of people, usually by violence or the threat of violence.

United Nations (UN) An international organization established in 1945 that brings all the world's powers together on international issues.

West Side Boys An armed group in Sierra Leone that held captive a West African peacekeeping force in 2000.

FOR MORE INFORMATION

Federal Emergency Management Agency
FEMA: Terrorism

P.O. Box 10055
Hyattsville, MD 20782-7055
http://www.fema.gov/hazard/terrorism/index.shtm
The Federal Emergency Management Agency is the United States' center for handling emergencies. Their Web page offers a thorough explanation of the different kinds of terrorism.

The Historical Association
59a Kennington Park Road
London SE11 4JH
London, England
The Historical Association is an independent charity located in England devoted to the study of British history.

U.S. Department of State
Sierra Leone
2201 C Street NW
Washington, DC 20520
http://www.state.gov/r/pa/ei/bgn/5475.htm
The U.S. Department of State handles diplomatic affairs, including relations with Sierra Leone.

Web Sites

Due to the changing nature of Internet links, Rosen Publishing has developed an online list of Web sites related to the subject of this book. This site is updated regularly. Please use this link to access the list:

http://www.rosenlinks.com/raid/wafr

FOR FURTHER READING

Beah, Ishmael. *A Long Way Gone: Memoirs of a Boy Soldier*. New York, NY: Farrar, Straus and Giroux, 2008.

Blin, Arnaud. *The History of Terrorism: From Antiquity to Al Qaeda*. Berkeley, CA: University of California Press, 2007.

Burleigh, Michael. *Blood and Rage: A Cultural History of Terrorism*. New York, NY: Harper Perennial, 2010.

Burton, Fred. *Ghost: Confessions of a Counterterrorism Agent*. New York, NY: Random House, 2009.

Clarence, C. *Understanding Terrorism: Challenges, Perspectives, and Issues*. Thousand Oaks, CA: Sage Publications, 2009.

Gberie, Lansana. *A Dirty War in West Africa: The RUF and the Destruction of Sierra Leone*. Bloomington, IN: Indiana University Press, 2005.

Griffin, P. D. *Encyclopedia of Modern British Army Regiments*. Charleston, SC: The History Press, 2007.

Hastings, Max. *The British Army: The Definitive History of the Twentieth Century*. London, England: Cassell Illustrated, 2008.

Hoffman, Bruce. *Inside Terrorism*. New York, NY: Columbia University Press, 2006.

Jones, Tim. *SAS Zero Hour: The Secret Origins of the Special Air Service*. Annapolis, MD: U.S. Naval Institute Press, 2006.

Myriam, Denov. *Child Soldiers: Sierra Leone's Revolutionary United Front*. New York, NY: Cambridge University Press, 2010.

O'Neill, Bard E. *Insurgency and Terrorism: From Revolution to Apocalypse*. Dulles, VA: Potomac Books, 2005.

Simonsen, Clifford E., and Jeremy R. Spindlove. *Terrorism Today: The Past, The Players, The Future*. 4th Edition. Upper Saddle River, NJ: Prentice Hall, 2009.

Stewart, Gary, and John Amman. *Black Man's Grave: Letters From Sierra Leone*. Berkeley Springs, WV: Cold Run Books, 2007.

BIBLIOGRAPHY

Collins, Tim, *Rules of Engagement* (Headline Books Publishing, London 2005)

Connaughton, Richard, *Operation 'Barras' in Small Wars & Insurgencies,* Vol. 12, No. 2(Frank Cass, Summer 2001)

Fowler, William, *Operation Barras* (Weidenfeld & Nicolson, London 2004)

Globe & Laurel (July /August, September/ October 2000)

Jane's Defence Glossary (Jane's Information Group, Coulsdon, UK 1993)

Jane's Geopolitical Library (Jane's Information Group, Coulsdon, UK 2000)

Lewis, Damien, *Operation Certain Death* (Century, London 2004)

Pegasus, The Yearbook (2000)

Pegasus (Winter 2000)

Soldier, Vol. 58, No. 10 (October 2000)

Windfall Films, SAS the Real Story, Channel 4

INDEX

ABOUT THE AUTHOR

Will Fowler has worked in journalism and publishing since 1972, reporting for European, American, Asian, and Arabic magazines from Europe, the USA, the Middle East, China and Southeast Asia. A Territorial Army soldier for 30 years, he was commissioned from the ranks in 4th Battalion Royal Green Jackets and volunteered for Operation Granby in the Gulf from 1990 to 1991. In 1993 he graduated from the French Army reserve staff officers course at the Ecole Militaire, Paris. Will is married and lives in Romsey, Hampshire, England.